Praise for *The S*

'The Secret Army ... roles. Gina's
method uncovers ... follow...but
those that do are n ... ompanies.'

- Joe Pulizzi, F ... uthor of five
  books includ. ... *...sinesses are Turning*
  Marketing Cost

'I love this book. Gina nas a style, an approach and a simplicity like no-one else I have ever read.'

- David Taylor, Founder and Author of *The Naked Leader*

'Here's what clear thinking and elegant writing can get you: *The Secret Army* delivers one of the most comprehensive and impressive leadership books I've read since *Good to Great*. You don't have time *not* to read this book and you should read it more than once.'

- Dain Dunston, Author of *The Downside of Up*, and co-author of *Nanovation, How a Little Car Can Teach The World to Think Big and Act Bold*

'It looks like a book on marketing, on business leadership, but at heart it's a book about people. About modern life. About corporate life. About *living*, not just surviving, in the modern world. It's engaging, at times funny, also serious, and darned useful. Having read it, I've found myself relating anecdotes to friends and family, whether they work in the corporate world or not. So much in the book is relatable to anyone who has had experience in business at any level, really.'

- Laurel Kriegler, Editor

'This marketer sure understands salespeople and leadership. I enjoyed this book and I think you will too.'

- Jeffrey J. Fox, Author of *How to Become a Rainmaker*

'Read it, loved it. It really resonates.'

- Ben Gale, Director of Criterion Quality Management

'It's brilliant. Thought provoking and entertaining with useful tips too.'

  Simon Robson, Business Development Executive at SMA Worldwide

ABOUT THE AUTHOR

Gina Balarin is a passionate corporate storyteller. She is the author of dozens of B2B case studies and hundreds of blog posts, and speaks regularly on panel discussions and at marketing conferences. She counts herself lucky to have done a TEDx talk, and chalks it up to having been on stage in various guises over the years, doing everything from being a magician's assistant and performing lead roles in ballet and drama productions, to representing companies as a Marketing Director at events.

She has a Master's Degree in Education in the subject of Management Communication, is a Chartered Marketer and Member of the Chartered Institute of Marketing, has a BA (Hons) in Linguistics and English Language, and a BA in Drama and Linguistics.

She's the author of this book and an unpublished romantic fiction novel, as well as many poems that no-one except her gets to read.

She loves connecting with people, so look her up and send her a personalised invite on LinkedIn. She's looking forward to hearing from you, especially if you've already bought a copy of this book.

Connect via: www.linkedin.com/in/ginabalarin/
or email: comments@the-secret-army-book.com

THE
SECRET
ARMY

LEADERSHIP, MARKETING AND THE POWER OF PEOPLE

Gina Balarin

Publisher's note

Every possible effort has been made to ensure that the information contained in this book is accurate at the time of going to press, and the publishers and author cannot accept responsibility for any errors or omissions, however caused. No responsibility for loss or damage occasioned to any person acting, or refraining from action, as a result of the material in this publication can be accepted by the editor, the publisher or the author.

CONTENTS

SECTION 5: MARKETERS AND SALESPEOPLE – THE LOVERS AND THE FIGHTERS

173

SECTION 1

THE SECRET ARMY: A WEAPON OF MASS DESTRUCTION OR MASS SUCCESS

Introduction

At first glance, this seems like a book about business leadership with a marketing angle. It is. But it's more than that. At heart it's a book about people, about modern life, about corporate life; about *living*, not just *surviving* at work.

It's about hidden idea-generators and the marketing striptease, relationship counselling for sales and marketing, secret influencers and the power of your customers, your employees and your leaders to really make a difference in your business.

This book is about connecting the power of language, philosophy, emotion, communication and motivation at work. It's about understanding what makes people 'tick'. It just happens to have a chapter or two about how marketing can help make all this a reality.

It is, as far as I know, the first book that looks at the power that marketing has *in combination with* leadership, employees and customers to make people happier, as well as make businesses better, while providing practical guidance and quirky insights into what happens when things go wrong.

This book has been called 'one of the most comprehensive and impressive leadership books... since Good to Great.' It wasn't written with this aim in mind, but rather to find the answer to this simple question: what makes a business compelling? Compelling to its employees, its customers, and its leaders – in other words, to its Secret Army.

It's a way of combining the power of people with the power of leadership and the power of storytelling in a single book – to pull together an ideology that should resonate with an audience of people who know that life is about more than just work: it's about meaning.

Written in five sections, this book addresses these key themes:

- What is the secret army, and what potential does it have for huge success or subversive destruction?
- What is leadership, and what does it mean to those touched by both great and terrible leadership?

- How can people who want to become leaders, but don't believe in their own potential, learn from others' mistakes and have the confidence to do what needs to be done to lead people into a new, scary world?
- What are the secret resources great leaders use today, but aren't even aware they use?
- How can people work together more effectively to make a difference every day in their work and home lives?
- What if marketing and sales could see the world from a different perspective, each other's and their customers'?

Some chapters are foundational in nature:

They summarise certain key concepts to give readers a sense of the basics, or a different way of looking at a subject they might assume they already know about.

- Chapter 3 covers fundamentals of marketing and the change in marketing over time.
- Chapter 7 talks about vision and strategy.
- Chapter 9 talks about leadership.
- Chapter 13 talks about managing change.
- Chapter 16 covers the voice of the customer.

If you're an expert in any of these areas, you may want to skim-read or skip these chapters. However, almost every chapter illuminates these concepts with real-life examples to turn theory into practice.

Some chapters are seemingly whimsical:

- Chapter 8 looks at the power truth-tellers have, when they're listened to.
- Chapter 9 talks about butterflies in a box and absentee landlords.
- Chapter 10 reveals frustrated storytellers and how much hidden marketing talent there really is lying around.
- Chapter 11 explains the power of undiscovered idea-generators.

- Chapter 12 explains who leaders really listen to – the hidden influencers, or the CEO's neck.
- Chapter 14 explains what a team chameleon is, why they make such good leaders and what this has to do with pre-competing.
- Chapter 15 covers the marketing striptease.

And other chapters, well, they're there for you to explore, discover and enjoy.

As you read on, you'll find stories about what trees, drama and the 5 Whys have in common with The Secret Army. You'll discover what an 'itch' is and why it's important to harness your own itch as well as those of your employees. You'll realise why humans are programmed to be social, discover the ROI on fun, and come across thoughts on dishwashers and winter coats, free mugs and customer lifetime value. You may even shed a tear when reading a story about what happens when leaders leave, or feel relieved to realise that everyone knows someone who's always 'doing something' (but never actually finishing it).

Along the way, you'll be in the company of great authors and thinkers, quoted throughout, and compelling leaders whose stories and lessons have inspired this book.

What are you waiting for? Read on.

Chapter 1: We Are Not Alone

Who makes up your Secret Army? In this chapter, we introduce the key players and talk about why great leaders produce supportive teams, why leaders eat last, and what happens when leaders are in or out of alignment with their companies and their teams.

Imagine you are surrounded by a Secret Army of like-minded individuals. These people buoy you up when you feel low, help you out when you are struggling, and keep you on the right path.

In great companies, as in our day-to-day lives, being part of a team can sometimes be like this. It can almost feel like there is an army of people who thinks like you do, acts in the 'right' way, and is focused on the same goals. But in other companies, life is not so grand. Everyone seems to be working towards a different aim. Salespeople blame marketing for not producing the right kinds of leads. Research and Development blames Production for not converting their visions into reality. Leadership blames employees for not 'getting it' or 'acting in the right way', or just for being bloody stupid and bloody-minded.

So, what's the difference? What's the secret that makes a Secret Army successful? And why go as far as to call it an 'army'?

GREAT LEADERSHIP BEGETS SUPPORTIVE TEAMS

Have you been in a situation where putting yourself second or consistently going out of your way to help someone was the norm, not because you were asked to do so, but because you wanted to? If so, something strong but invisible was probably driving this behaviour. You might not have thought much about it at the time – we seldom do – but it's human nature to make these kinds of sacrifices when we trust others to do the same for us. Regardless of whether it happened in your work or personal life, if you stop to think about it, you'll probably find that you were surrounded by a supportive group of people at the time. And while you were putting yourself second, others were doing the same for you too.

Occasionally, when people are in environments where they work well with others, they give without counting the cost, almost without thinking.

This selfless mentality is one of the secrets of great teamwork. When leaders eat last, something extraordinary occurs... the team makes sure there's enough for their leaders to eat too!

I've seen it happen, both as a follower and as a leader. I once had a boss who was going through a hard time. Her long-term relationship had broken up, she had to move house, and there were even custody issues over her cat. But she had built a team that had each other's backs, no matter what. So, when the chips were down, we were there. We made sure our team never missed a deadline, a meeting or let project timelines slip. After all, she'd been doing the same for us for years. Supporting our leader when she needed it was, quite frankly, never in question – we didn't even think twice about it.

Years later, I experienced what it was like to be in her shoes – to be the leader who always had to be strong, have all the answers, provide leadership and guidance – and who just didn't have the capacity to do it any longer. And something amazing happened: my team did the same thing for me. I discovered that, whether it's solving a particularly challenging problem or just helping out in whatever way they can (from making very necessary and welcome cups of tea to motivating the rest of the team to take on whatever responsibilities they can), the team actually becomes its own body of self-leadership if, or when, a leader is incapacitated.

This is the idea behind the concept that leaders eat last. It isn't just a catchy phrase; it comes from a real life military environment. In this context, in contrast to many class- or wealth-focused societies, higher-ranking individuals don't benefit from their privileges of rank. In mess halls, leaders *actually do* eat last.[a] Instead of forcing the newest or lowliest

---

[a] It has been the norm in the British Army for more than seventy years and is what Sandhurst, the elite British Military academy, describes as 'officers eat last' in alignment with their motto 'Serve to Lead.'

recruits to wait at the back of the line for their daily victuals, leaders wait until their entire team has been served first. And if there isn't enough food to go around, they simply don't eat.

It doesn't just work for the British Army, though. It works for the Secret Army in business and personal life, and underpins this simple philosophy: great leadership begets great teams. When leaders eat last, their teams recognise this fact. They know that sacrifices are worth making and that someone 'has their back'. As a result, team-members will go to extraordinary lengths for leaders who they feel deserve their support.

This kind of selfless support is earned, not demanded.

On the other hand, megalomaniacal leaders, selfish leaders, and leaders who achieve their aims through fear or tyranny may certainly command an army, achieve objectives and deliver results. But at what cost? The long-term impacts of bad leadership wreak havoc on more than businesses. They can wreck lives too.

I've worked in too many businesses with weak or failing leadership, and come away with a feeling that I have somehow been inadequate, stupid or a failure – only to discover (usually much later) that I wasn't the only employee who felt that way. Only after open, honest discussions with people who worked for the same companies at the same time have I discovered that I wasn't the problem: the problem was almost too big to see. The problem lay with the company not realising the huge potential at their disposal – they couldn't, wouldn't, or didn't know how to leverage this potential. They didn't understand the human capacity for excellence. They didn't realise that while armies of old marched on their stomachs, the modern business army marches on its gut instincts.

MARCHING ON YOUR 'GUTS'

Modern psychological studies[1] have identified a link between what goes on in our heads, hearts or brains (i.e. psychological factors) and how symptoms manifest themselves in our bodies (i.e. physical factors). It's no coincidence that phrases like 'a pain in the neck' or 'a gut reaction' have entered our lexicon. Work can, literally, be a pain in the neck. I worked with someone who constantly came up against challenges with the head of the company and then noticed he was developing severe neck pain. When we discussed it, we realised that his stressful interactions with the head of the company were the root cause of his neck pain, which, incidentally, disappeared shortly after he left the job.

This example is anecdotal, but the cost of being 'out of alignment' with your company has actually been measured in terms of productivity and financial costs. According to the Health and Safety Executive, the total amount of working time lost due to work-related stress, anxiety and depression in 2015/16 was 11.7 million days.[2] In 2015/16, stress accounted for 37 per cent of all work-related ill-health cases, and 45 per cent of all working days lost due to ill health. In 2013, a study by leading psychiatrists found that more than 8 million men, women and children suffer from anxiety disorders a year – at a cost to the UK of £9.8 billion.[3] Costs will only have increased since then. Indeed, Anxiety UK's 2016 Facts and Stats report that '244,000+ new cases of work related stress, depression or anxiety were diagnosed in the UK in 2015 – that's 668 a day or one every 2.1 minutes'.[4,b]

So, if our bodies manifest our mental states, what happens when our instincts, intuition and emotions are either in alignment with business goals, or in contrast?

IN ALIGNMENT

Concur is a company where employees are encouraged to 'live a big life'. Started by two brothers (Raj and Steve Singh) and their mate (Mike Hilton) in a rented flat, the company grew over twenty years to have around five thousand employees by the time it was sold to SAP in 2014. When I joined, in 2012, the CEO and his brother still sincerely made

---

[b] For more in-depth analysis, take a look at http://www.hse.gov.uk/STATISTICS /causdis/stress/stress.pdf

an attempt to meet every single new employee who joined the business. I was fortunate enough to have breakfast with Raj Singh at an induction conference for new starters, where we chatted about kids, holidays and bicycles; I even danced with Steve at one end-of-year company function (he insisted he couldn't dance, but I wouldn't take no for an answer and he was much better on the dance floor than he gave himself credit for!). When I was head-hunted for a role that forced me to leave Concur, a company where I felt I had found my 'work home', it took me three months to decide to leave. This was extraordinary, as I was only on a one-month notice period at the time.

What Raj, Steve, Mike, and the whole management team they employed, did was create something special. They founded a company with a clear vision, an effective strategy, and, above all, a heart. For them, having a vision of 'the death of the expense report' wasn't just a reason to make money (and they certainly *did* make money out of it – a lot of money! In 2014 they sold Concur to SAP for $8.3 billion); it was more like a mission.

They knew that modern business success comes from hiring intelligent, like-minded individuals with passion, and they actively recruited a group of people who had guts, brains and heart. They knew, very well, the power of their Secret Army, and how to use this Secret Army to work for them and with them. Their modern army of marketers, salesmen and women, R&D creators, managers, developers and innovators marched on their guts.

OUT OF ALIGNMENT

Have you ever worked in a job you hated? Most of us have, at some point in time. I've had jobs I dreaded so much that I'd be physically sick each morning before I left for work. I've had friends who worked at places where they were so miserable that they couldn't face getting out of bed to go to work. Another friend, who was normally in perfect health, was so unhappy and stressed in his job that it took him getting shingles (the grown-up version of chicken pox – highly contagious and also not something you get unless you're *really* run down) to finally realise he had to chuck it in.

More and more of us live 'lives of quiet desperation'. It's no surprise that depression rates have soared. The World Health Organisation says that, 'globally, more than 300 million people of all ages suffer from depression'.[5] According to Healthline,[6] one in ten Americans are reportedly affected by depression at any given moment. Even more significantly, the number of patients diagnosed with depression increases by approximately 20 per cent per year. Anxiety UK[7] reports that 40 per cent of disability worldwide is due to depression and anxiety, and in 2014 it was 'estimated that one in six people in the past week experienced a common mental health problem'.[8] Much of this is job-related stress.

The thing is, we don't have to carry on living this way. Our culture, which is increasingly competitive, stressful, busy and unceasing, also shows bright spots[9] – moments of enlightenment or brilliance. In this context, I'm talking about the bright spots of increasing cultural awareness about the scourge of stress and mental illness.

One of my favourite examples is the advertising campaign run by CALM – the Campaign Against Living Miserably. This British organisation is dedicated to raising awareness of the shockingly high suicide rate of men[c], and they do this by running outdoor advertising campaigns – specifically, bus stop adverts.[10] They created a #ManDictionary with adverts ranging from the humorous to the downright sobering. Examples include: 'MANTIHERO – noun/ dude with problems who we all root for', and 'MANDOWN – one of the twelve men who take their life every day in this country'.

But this problem is not just limited to men, nor is it exclusive to people in the UK. It's a global problem – and one that great companies are aware of and are looking to resolve.

Arguably, the problem may stem from a general cultural lack of purpose. One solution is for great companies and

---

[c] In 2014, male suicide accounted for 76 per cent of all suicides and was the single biggest cause of death in men under the age of 45 in the UK.

great leaders to give a sense of purpose to their employees and, in so doing, build their own Secret Army of followers who can help their teammates and leaders alike cope when times are tough.

The employees in your company no longer come to work, do the job, and go home as they did in years gone by. If people are dissatisfied enough, they simply won't want to work for you any longer; and they'll let their friends know.

In fact, your employees now have the ability to make, or destroy, your company.

This is both the benefit and the disadvantage of Glassdoor,[11] the online platform that lets people see the company's and senior management's ratings *before* they apply for the job. It works brilliantly for a company when the ratings are good, but it can work against them when a few dissatisfied, but vocal, employees speak out in this public forum rather than choosing (or feeling able) to resolve issues internally.

WHO IS THE SECRET ARMY?

The Secret Army that can make or break your company isn't just the group of people leading your company; it's also your employees, your customers, and advocates from the general public who speak about your brand with affection, respect or admiration. They may not even be customers... yet... but they admire what you do and, by sharing the word, make your brand more desirable and therefore make sales more likely.

As leaders, you need to harness your employees' strengths so that they make your company greater than the sum of its parts rather than the unpleasant and unprofitable alternative. As employees, you need to be brave enough to speak your mind internally as well as externally, and, as customers, honesty is important too.

Whether you are a customer, an employee or a manager, this book is about understanding the Secret Army almost better than you understand yourself, so that you can conquer your enemy, however you define it, and lead your company to victory.

A NOTE ABOUT THIS BOOK'S STRUCTURE

As we proceed through the book, we'll conclude each chapter with a selection of key takeways that summarise the chapter's core points. Each chapter after this one also contains a lesson that you can apply directly to your business life.

Key Takeaways:

- *While armies of old marched on their stomachs, the modern business army marches on its guts.*

- *Great leaders support their teams and, in turn, are supported by them when the chips are down – this is the key philosophy underpinning The Secret Army.*

- *It's important for companies, leaders and employees to be in alignment. The result of not being aligned is that individuals' health, the bottom line, and the company as a whole could suffer.*

- *Your employees have the ability to make, or destroy, your company.*

Chapter 2: Your Employees

Why are your employees such a critical part of your Secret Army? What do they really need, and how can you keep them on your side? In this chapter, we answer these questions, discuss why we're programmed to be social, consider whether money is or isn't a motivator, and investigate how to have autonomy, mastery and purpose over our work.

WHAT DO PEOPLE NEED?

The psychologist Abraham Maslow is the author of a famously-quoted illustration: the hierarchy of needs. Starting with the most basic needs – physiological (food, water, clothing, a place to sleep) and safety, he moves on to the need for love/belonging, then esteem, and finally 'self-actualisation' (meeting your full potential).[12]

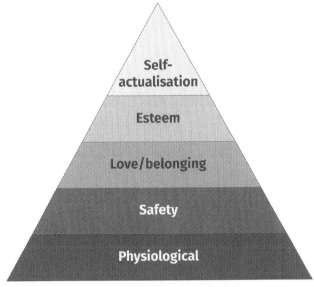

Maslow's Hierarchy of Needs

If you live in an industrialised nation with a good GDP and have either a job or a means of social support, your basic needs are likely to be met.[d] But the needs of love/belonging, esteem and self-actualisation are what makes a difference between living and *being alive*.

One can argue that it's up to individuals to meet their own needs – that it's not the responsibility of companies to create fully fulfilled individuals or to keep them that way. However, that's exactly what great companies *do*.

Great companies aren't just about the money. Or, at least, that's not the force that drives them. No matter whether their business exists to help people, to save the world, to create a new and brilliant product or to make life easier – they have a reason for existing. It's often called their 'why'.

So how does this relate to the Secret Army in your business? It's simple, really. People need to know WHY you do it. It is no longer enough for employees to simply work for a company in exchange for a pay cheque. They expect more. They demand more. And their psychology now requires more. People are increasingly becoming sick precisely because of this disconnect between high expectations (society's and their own) and either their perceived inability to meet these expectations or their frustrations at not being able to be more, do more or have more.

What great companies do, however, is understand what drives their Secret Army. It's what great generals have done since the dawn of time. It's what Sun Tzu wrote about in *The Art of War*.[13] This philosophy of 'know your enemy better than you know yourself' applies to your Secret Army, i.e. your employees and your customers.

WE'RE PROGRAMMED TO BE SOCIAL

People are human. We have human needs and human desires, and, according to Matthew D. Lieberman, we are innately programmed to be social[14] – that is, to think about other people, how they perceive us, how we integrate with each

---

[d] These days, internet access / Wi-Fi is half-jokingly referred to as a basic human need. In fact, an article by David Kravets of Wired reported on 6 March 2011 that 'U.N. report declares internet access a human right'.

other, and how we collaborate. That's what differentiates groups of animals with a higher level of intelligence from the 'lizard brains' of reptiles. It's in our genetic makeup to connect with other humans. Human babies cry when they're distressed, and humans respond instinctively to those cries. In fact, the social attention or grooming that humans receive from their parents and peers has been shown, in studies, to give us opioid-linked pleasure responses in the brain. In other words, it makes us feel good. We need social connections. Lieberman says that as humans, we tend to do verbal rather than physical grooming. So, when people spend time verbally 'grooming' us, it's a sign that we are safe and cared for.

In the office environment, however, with the increasingly stringent requirement to deliver results at almost any cost, this human need for social connection is being ignored. But, from an evolutionary perspective, forming cohesive social connections with others is critical. Those social connections are the difference between being part of a team and simply doing a job. Humans actually have a biological need for social collaboration.

It has been said that if you have a job you love, you'll never work another day in your life.[e] This is what great companies, with great leaders, know intuitively. Give your employees a reason to come to work every day and they'll stop watching the clock. It's this passion that creates great companies in the first place. It's easy to see this passion in evidence in entrepreneurs who start a company, believe in it and grow it. Their passion is infectious.

One great example is Patrick Drake, co-founder of HelloFresh – the recipe box service that sends out more than 8.5 million meals per month. His passion for great food led him to turn away from earning a great income as a lawyer to start up HelloFresh, which is now hugely successful.

---

[e] This quote has been attributed variously to the Chinese philosopher Confucius, Marc Antony and Mark Twain – which one was it really? Here's more info: https://quoteinvestigator.com/2014/09/02/job-love/

He insists you should 'make sure you have a mission and a purpose from the beginning, and infuse everything you do in the business with it. That's why customers will buy in to what you're doing.'[15]

On the other hand, if people feel like they're just a cog in a machine – and that the machine they're working for is turning out a product they really don't care about – it's easy to become disillusioned. A friend of mine who once worked in an incredibly mindless job, which she eventually left, said what I think many of us have often thought: 'We spend the vast majority of our waking lives at work. Therefore it is far better to enjoy the work you do than to be miserable.'

> You need a supportive management team, an atmosphere of trust, and employees must have the freedom to be innovative. From experience, it helps to provide people with the tools they need to do their job as simply and easily as possible.
>
> – Henry Stewart

I couldn't agree more.

Great companies know this, intuitively. Others simply believe that paying people enough – or, perhaps, even quite well – is sufficient to keep them motivated. It's not.

MONEY ISN'T THE ONLY MOTIVATOR

Somewhat counterintuitively for HR directors, who believe that employees are financially-focused, recent research[16] has shown that employees actually want a good manager and opportunities for progression and training, *far more than they want a pay increase*. Here's an extract from the article to illustrate this point:

> Too often, companies seek to win the talent war by throwing ever more money into the mix... By applying sophisticated data analytics, a key finding rose to the fore: employees in smaller teams, with longer periods between promotions

and with lower-performing managers, were more likely to leave.

Once these high-risk employees had been identified, more informed efforts were made to convince them to stay. Chiefly, these involved greater opportunities for learning development and more support from a stronger manager. Bonuses, on the other hand, proved to have little if any effect. As a result, funds that might have been allocated to ineffectual compensation increases were instead invested in learning development for employees and improved training for managers. Performance and retention both improved, with significant savings left over.

It took big data analysis of the internal HR records for the major US insurer quoted in this article to confirm what great leaders have always known: give people a purpose, help them find their own way to turn that purpose into reality, and you have a winning formula for success.

Another example comes from Dan Ariely[17] in his book *Predictably Irrational: The Hidden Forces That Shape Our Decisions*, as summarised by James Wilkinson:

Dan Ariely is the James B. Duke Professor of Psychology and Behavioural Economics at Duke University, and has done many studies into the nature of motivation. My favourite is the one he did at an Intel factory in Israel, where they split employees into four groups. Three groups were offered incentives to increase their productivity each day, consisting of either cash, pizza or a compliment from their boss. The fourth was offered nothing in order to create a control group. The employees were making computer chips, which made the results easy to measure.

Which group do you think was more productive? On the first day it was pizza, with compliments a close second. By the end of the experiment, the compliments had edged in, but those two were very close. What was shocking though, was that the group who were offered a cash incentive performed worse than the control group, meaning that offering a cash incentive was worse than no incentive at all!

By the end of the week, the compliment proved to be the best motivator. In addition, 'the cash bonus cost the company more *and* resulted in a 6.5 per cent drop in productivity.'[18]

The irony is that giving compliments and pizza, investing in learning and development, and understanding how people place a value beyond money on their roles is already instinctive for any team-focused manager who knows that people are people, not money-making machines.

A few years ago, I was fortunate enough to interview 'Happy Henry' for a blog post about employee satisfaction. Henry Stewart, author of *The Happy Manifesto*,[19] said this about money: 'Forty-eight per cent of the population would take a pay cut to have a different manager – they value their work life and how well they are treated more highly than their salary. People want to be paid well and deserve to be paid well, but it's more important to have a good, supportive environment to work in.'

The great thing is that having a good, supportive environment saves the company money – a lot of money, and it makes people happier. What's not to love?

WHAT MAKES A GREAT WORKPLACE?

What Henry touches on here is brilliantly summarised in Daniel Pink's book *Drive: The Surprising Truth About What Motivates Us*.[20] It's well worth reading the book, but to summarise it, these are the key elements. People need to be given enough independence to do what they're good at doing (autonomy), they need to be able to work towards becoming a master of their field (mastery), and they need to have a purpose for doing what they do in the first place. We'll cover this in more detail in Chapter 5.

CAN BUSINESSES (...)
MASTERY AND PURP(...)

Let's not kid ourselves ar(...)
have a lot on their plate. (...)
that sells, they need a w(...)
price it right, find custo(...)
and – ultimately – make a(...)

But they cannot do (...)
without an army of indiv(...)
and keep them on track e(...)

The only way to ensu(...)
will step in and carry the (...)
done, is to give them a rea(...)
day. It starts by giving them autonomy, opportunities for mastery, and a sense of purpose. Great companies are able to do this – to make people feel like they're not just a lowly cog in a machine. It not only goes a long way towards gaining their support, it also makes them feel great – because by doing what they do, and doing it well, they help the wheels of their industry turn.

> **LESSON 1:** Your employees are the largest regiment in your Secret Army. Most of them *want* to do a good job. Treating them like human beings is good for them, and good for business.

Key Takeaways:

- Forming cohesive soci(...)
  Those social connect(...)
  of a team, and si(...)
- Being train(...)
  increase(...)
- 'If(...)

connections with others is critical.
ⁿns are the difference between being part
ₚly doing a job.

ⁿd and working for a better manager, not salary
, make people want to stay at a job for longer.

ⁿou have a job that you love, you'll never work another day
ⁿn your life.' Give your employees a reason to come to work
every day and they'll stop watching the clock.

- The only way to ensure that a helpful, supportive army will
  step in and carry the weight of the work that needs to be done,
  is to give them a reason to want to come to work every day.

- Giving your employees – the largest regiment of your Secret
  Army – a sense of why they come to work could make the
  difference between them existing and them feeling truly alive.

- People need to be given enough independence to do what
  they're good at doing (autonomy), they need to be able to
  work towards becoming a master of their field (mastery),
  and they need to have a purpose for doing what they do in
  the first place.

Chapter 3: Your Customers

Should you sleep with your customers? In this chapter, we answer this question with an example, and discuss whether marketing personas are meaningful or just box-ticking exercises. We consider the hidden advantage of truly knowing your customers, and the fundamental shift of marketing over time. Bearing current marketing trends in mind, we look at the ladder of loyalty, why your customers' stories are now the biggest weapon available to your Secret Army, and the importance of social proof.

HOW WELL DO YOU KNOW YOUR CUSTOMERS?

No, really. Be honest. Would you sleep with them if you could?

There's a TEDx talk by Simone Vincenzi[21] provocatively entitled 'Sleeping with your customers'. No, it's not about the colloquial definition of the phrase 'sleep with'. Or, if he did engage in any 'ahem' kinds of activities with his customers, he certainly didn't disclose it during his presentation. No. Instead, it's about spending time with your customers, living in each other's office space – or, indeed, renting space together – so that you can get to know your customers' needs better than you know your own.

Simone actually did sleep with his customers. He shared office and living space with them. He ate with them, slept in the same place as them, worked with them. It was a kind of social experiment – and it paid off. By spending even more time together than most people would with their spouse, he got to know his customers in new, unique and surprising ways. He started to understand their challenges, their joys and triumphs, their tribulations, their frustrations – and it made him better at his job as a result.

Something weird also came out of such an unnaturally close relationship... his customers got to know him better too. As a result, they were more understanding when deadlines had to be moved or things weren't on track to be delivered in the way they had anticipated. Together, they built a journey of mutual comprehension – and the destination was much sweeter as a result.

So, let me ask again – how well do you really know your customers?

There's a current marketing trend called 'persona creation'. The idea is to research your typical customers, identify their common needs and desires, and put them into buckets. I both love and hate personas. They're great if they really help your business to understand:

- why people buy from you,
- the needs you're meeting that you didn't know you were meeting,
- the needs you think you're meeting, but aren't, or, better still,
- the *real* reason they buy from you.

But there's a risk, as with all trendy marketing tools, that, rather than creating meaningful descriptions of your customers by truly understanding them, the personas simply become a box-ticking exercise. There's a risk that creating a persona does three things:

- it turns real people into caricatures of themselves,
- it makes you miss the individual understanding of what really makes them tick, and
- it makes you lazy.

WHAT IS A PERSONA?

Let me explain with an example. Imagine that you sell software to heads of finance. Your persona might be called 'the CFO' or, perhaps, 'Richard'. You know that he has a budget of X, his focus activities are driving down costs, increasing profitability and making the numbers look good to the board. His hobbies are playing golf. He has children. He lives in a five bedroom house and his busiest times are at month-end, the end of financial quarter, and year-end.

Perhaps you've even given him a 'photo' to identify him. He wears an expensive suit, an open-necked collared shirt, shiny shoes, is greying at the temples and looks wise (and perhaps just a little bit stressed).

That's great! You know who Richard is now, don't you?

I'm willing to bet that you still haven't the foggiest clue. Have you identified what Richard's hopes and dreams are? Do you know what his ambitions are for his company, and for his diverse role within the company? Do you know what he is planning beyond this financial year, what makes him come alive, what the things are that he hates most? Probably not.

And that's the risk of not truly knowing your customers. You put them in a 'box' and talk to them like they're all the same, without ever *really* knowing what makes them tick.

Now, don't get me wrong. Personas are not a bad thing. They're a great way of helping companies (and marketing teams, specifically) realise who their customers are. And they're a great way of building the discipline of talking to a single target audience (i.e. CFO Richard) at a time. They're a great tool for trying to get to grips with what your customers want and how you can solve their problems, and they're useful for helping marketers understand who the players are in the decision-making process (especially when your business has long or complex sales cycles, or where multiple stakeholders are involved – as in many business-to-business companies). Personas should also help anyone who is involved in the marketing or sales process think harder about whether they're giving the right messages to the right people.

A PERSONA IS NOT NEARLY ENOUGH

If you want to really understand the value of your company's product or service, the best advice I could ever give to any new person coming into a marketing department is this: don't just rely on personas and assume they're the truth, the whole truth and nothing but the truth (it makes for lazy marketing). Instead, make friends with your sales team and your account managers. Ask them what their sales process is. Ask them who your customers are and what makes them come alive, what problems your product or service is solving for them now, and what their future challenges are likely to be. Ask them what they need to make it easier to sell your product or service to prospective customers. And then do it. Because your salespeople *do* (or at least, should) understand your customers better than anyone else.

And the best advice I could offer to business leaders is this: just because you've probably been there, done that and bought the t-shirt when it comes to selling your product or service; and just because you assume that no-one knows the business better than you do (especially if you're in a very senior position), *doesn't mean you're right!* Markets change. Customers change. Their needs change. Their motivations change. Customers are human. And, at the end of the day, you're never just selling what you think you're selling to your customers. You're actually selling something almost entirely nebulous. You're really selling a feeling.

PEOPLE BUY FROM PEOPLE

David Taylor wrote in *The Naked Leader*[22] that '[p]eople buy from people. People motivate, promote and sack people and, although our future is in our own hands, we need others to help us achieve it. How we interact with other human beings is critical to personal, team, and organisational success.'

So, what drives that success?

I like the way Jeffrey J. Fox[23] asks this question in his book about developing sales excellence, *How to Become a Rainmaker*: 'What is the single attribute… that distinguishes the markedly great salesperson from the merely good?'

If you're thinking things like 'hard work, the ability to listen, the ability to close a deal' etc. then you're halfway there. The answer is both more obvious and more frustrating than you might imagine. Fox says, 'The one thing that separates the number one salesperson from the rest is that the number one person *sells more.*'

Duh!

Or is it? Really, if you read the book, you discover that the number one salesperson (or rainmaker) sells more because they do their homework, they treat people with respect, they understand the problem the business is *really* trying to solve for their customers – and it's usually *not* just the product's benefits or features. How do they do this? They understand the customers' needs so well that they almost know their customers better than they know themselves.

Are you seeing a trend here? Good. The trend is that knowledge is power, and knowledge about the people who 'buy', or 'buy in', to your company's raison d'être gives you a hidden advantage.

In the previous chapter, we talked about how important it is to know your employees – what motivates them, what their human needs are, what makes them come alive – why you need to have a clear business purpose, share it with your employees, and why leaders will always serve themselves last (not first) at a meal. Now, imagine that your employees are that Secret Army that supports your business goals, helps you carry out your strategy and enables you to achieve your objectives. It's not difficult to imagine. You need them to deliver that product or service, build your business and 'win the war' for profit.

So, where do your customers come into the mix? So far in this chapter, we've discussed the importance of getting to know and understand them, but how do they form part of your Secret Army?

To answer this question, we'll take an apparent digression into the fundamental shifts in marketing over time, because the technology that has allowed marketing to evolve the way businesses communicate with their customers also tells a story about how likely people are to engage with marketing messages, trust them and let them influence their buying decisions.

Marketing through the ages

- 1950s – This was the age of spin: the 'Mad Men' used TV as the primary medium for influencing public opinion.
- 1960s – Here we entered the age of individuality and 'cola': the 'Pepsi Challenge' led to cola wars celebrating sharing, community and freedom.[24]
- 1970s – It's hard to summarise an entire decade of marketing with one phrase, but 'I'd like to buy the world a Coke' is probably a great way of thinking about the pervasiveness of big brands and their influence on society in this decade.[25]
- 1980s – The 80s ushered in the age of the telephone (and caller ID).
- 1990s – We welcomed the age of email, the dawn of 'mass personalisation' and the use of the internet for marketing.
- 2000 – By the middle of the 'noughties' we were ready to usher in the age of social media, and started to realise the dawn of 'inbound marketing' – the idea that people come to you because you're providing them with value. This wouldn't have been possible without the internet and search engines!
- 2010 & beyond – We're now living in the age of storytelling, content, context and authenticity. There's so much information out there now that the only way to attract people is to understand who they are, what their problems are, and how our products/services can connect with them as human beings (even if we're selling to huge, apparently 'faceless' corporations).[f]

---

[f] This content is based on a presentation I gave in 2016. Stop lying to your customers! Marketing in the era of authenticity. Presentation at B2BMarketing Summit 2016. Retrieved 11 June 2017 from
https://www.b2bmarketing.net/en/events/summit-2016/key-takeaways-2016

ANOTHER WAY OF LOOKING AT THE EVOLUTION OF MARKETING

| Broadcast | Direct | Digital | Inbound | Emotional | Authentic |

An evolution of marketing

From this diagram, we can see that marketing went from mass sharing – with no possibility for feedback – to 'faking' individual attention via supposedly 'personalised' emails, to digital – where everything started going online. The inbound marketing philosophy embraced valuable content as a way of drawing people to your website or brand. But, while companies now have all these tools available at their fingertips to use as they see fit, I think that the true differentiators are still those that require people to get emotionally involved, to believe in a product. Not 'believe' in a naïve, 'drinking the Kool-Aid' kind of way (although there is sometimes an element of that, especially with charismatic brands that attract followers almost as if they were a religion), but 'believe' as in trust.

I think that we now live in an era of authenticity. It doesn't pay to lie – not initially and not in the long run. In fact, with the prevalence of social media, lying to your customers can actually be the early warning signs of your company's death knell if they find out the ugly truths you've been trying to hide.[8] It has happened to companies time and again – most notably in our recent history, the failure of the banks in the 2007/8 financial crisis. Lehman Brothers comes to mind. Before them, Enron crumbled spectacularly for similar unethical reasons.

---

[8] If you have further examples, please get in touch – the internet is surprisingly silent on this topic…

What this model of marketing tells us, though, is that we've moved from an era where consumers were assumed to be passive absorbers of knowledge who would purchase almost anything if it was advertised often enough, to an era where buyers are highly discerning, extremely critical, have very high standards and lack loyalty. If you piss them off, they'll simply move on to one of your competitors.

Or will they?

Actually, that's not quite the whole story. There's a commonly-referred to diagram called 'The ladder of loyalty' or 'The loyalty ladder', based on the original thinking by Philip Kotler, who is often referred to as the father of modern marketing.[h] Here, customers are placed on a ladder that marks their progression from 'suspect' to 'advocate'.

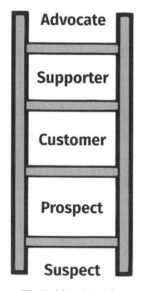

The Ladder of Loyalty

As they take a step up each rung of the ladder, it is assumed they'll get more and more delighted with the brand and, as a

---

[h] Although Philip did not design the ladder, his thinking on loyalty inspired it.

result, be more likely to speak persuasively to others about how convinced they are about the brand's value.

But, in my opinion, it isn't a linear progression. Indeed, one of the surprising facts about loyalty is that, sometimes, bad customer service, *when it is remedied in a more than satisfactory way*, can turn customers from doubters into advocates (or, at the very least, from 'mildly satisfied' to 'definitely delighted').

Examples abound, but I'll quote one from Jonah Berger's book *Contagious: how to build word of mouth in the digital age.*[26]

To summarise his story briefly, his cousin moved from California to the East Coast of the USA. From hot to cold. On his arrival, he bought a stylish coat that simply didn't cut the mustard when the temperature dropped below zero. So, he found a coat that looked a bit like a sleeping bag, but was 'warm enough to withstand even the coldest East Coast winter'. It wasn't cheap, but it worked. Until the zipper broke. He was infuriated and frustrated. It's just not possible to walk around in that kind of cold without the right coat. But when he called up Land's End (the manufacturer), this is what they said.

> 'Repair?' she asked. 'We'll just send you a new one in the mail.' 'How much will that cost?' my cousin asked nervously. 'It's free,' she replied, 'and we'll send it out two-day mail so you don't have to wait. It's too cold this winter to go out with a broken coat.'

Now that's a great example of how to turn your customer from a detractor (after all, his very expensive product had broken) into an advocate. It worked so well that his cousin wrote about it in his book (free publicity), and I'm quoting it here too. I'd never even heard of the brand before, by the way, but the story is so compelling that it's worth sharing. And that's why it's so important to realise that your customers have enormous power to keep your brand alive: it's not just by buying your products, it's by loving them – and helping others to love them too – that brings us to the next Secret Army lesson.

LESSON 2: Your customers are a critical part of your Secret Army – but they can work *for* or *against* you. They need proof to be convinced to stay on your side.

Every single purchasing decision – whether it's the relatively simple or mundane (buying a cup of coffee) or the long-term, expensive and commitment-heavy (investing in new software or buying a house) – is made based on some kind of proof.

Buyers do, obviously, buy from people they like – people who think like them, have the same values as them or are simply able to understand what they want (and then sell it to them). But they also need evidence. In our digital age, information is available everywhere about almost everything. Buying a tumble dryer is no longer a day-long task involving a trip to one or two stores, a discussion with a sales rep, a quick glance at the potential load size and a purchase on your credit card.

Nope.

Buying a tumble dryer is now nearly as complex as investing in your child's future education. Yes, there's the load size, but there's also the energy efficiency, the number of cycles, the tray for drying shoes, the drying speed, the machine dimensions, the colour, the weight, the discounts available and whether they will remove your old machine – for a fee or not for a fee. But that's not all. Today it can take weeks, or even months, to *properly* research a tumble dryer – after all, it's a ten-year investment if you get a good one. And it's incredibly, and increasingly, complex to make such a decision with the plethora of information available – it can simply be too much information, sometimes. Trust me, I know, from personal experience.

So, what do we do? We require social proof.

Yes, I will be swayed by the aforementioned factors, but what is finally going to convince me, one way or another, whether an investment is right for me or not? Social proof. That is, the stories other people tell about the products: how they worked for them and what problems they solved.

Amazon has done a lot for society – and, arguably, it's taken a lot away from us (patience, for one thing, and the ability of independent stores to compete on price) – but one of the things we really have to thank Amazon for is the rating/review feature associated with products.[i] Because, you see, what Amazon reviews allow users to do is to put their purchases in context, give them meaning, and help people believe that products will work. They also allow people to identify with how a product will make them feel.

If I'm trying to justify the investment in a tumble dryer that costs four times the price of its competitor, the features will impress me, but what will really sell me the product is the true story of the mum who doesn't think the child lock works quite brilliantly because her toddler keeps unlocking it (clever toddler!), or the guy who says his wife loves it and that's convincing enough for him. We have Amazon to thank for the personalisation of products, the humanisation of machinery, and the ability to empathise with individuals who have made the same choice we have – and been pleased with it.

Our customers' stories make our products and our services *real*. They provide the proof that our business has a reason to exist – because we solve problems for *real* people, people like our customers. That's why, when salespeople whinge that marketers haven't provided case studies in exactly the right market or for precisely the desired industry, they have a point. Customers need to be convinced by other people that they can be helped.

So, how do you make the best use of your customers?

---

[i] It's worth noting here that Amazon products have also been a victim of astroturfing and paid reviews. Although they try to crack down on these, unethical companies go a long way to 'cheat the system'. That's life, unfortunately.

TIPS TO REALLY UNDERSTAND YOUR CUSTOMERS

- Keep communicating with them in good times and bad.
- Tell them about the good things you're doing.
- Let them talk to people like themselves (other customers – this is why customer events are good for business).
- Get their honest feedback (and take action to fix the issues they raise).
- Help them put their words into a repeatable format – be that in a case study, a written testimonial, a short 'quote' or even a video.
- Always be on the lookout for new customer stories, and be ready to capture those stories when you come across them. (We'll talk more about this in Chapter 18.)

Key Takeaways:

- *Your customers are some of the most important members of your Secret Army. By getting to know them and how they think, everyone in the business benefits. Moreover, if you really understand who you're selling to and why they choose to buy, you can find ways of selling more, better.*

- *Marketing has changed fundamentally over time. We now live in an era of authenticity. Customers are highly discerning, extremely critical, have very high standards, and lack loyalty – unless you give them a reason to love you.*

- *It's possible to turn customers from being dissatisfied into brand advocates, but it means giving them more than they expect.*

- *Stories make or break the trust your buyers will have in your product or service. You have to get those social proof points from your customers, and case studies are an excellent way to do that.*

- *Our customers' stories make our products and our services* real. *They provide the proof that our business has a reason to exist.*

Chapter 4: Your Management Team

Who's in charge of your Secret Army? What difference does it make if they're managers or leaders? In this chapter, we address these issues, talk about what makes a true leader, and discuss what happens when true leaders leave a company. We include a snippet from Sun Tzu, and cover the importance of knowing where you're going.

TRUE LEADERSHIP

There are managers, and then there are leaders. Anyone who has ever been inspired by a leader will recognise leadership. On the other hand, anyone who has ever reported to a 'manage-by-results' manager will recognise management. Occasionally, the two separate talents combine into a glorious whole, and that's when the magic happens.

While Google's instant search results don't always provide truly insightful responses. I really liked the answer to my question, 'What's the difference between management and leadership?' that it came up with from go2HR,

> The main difference between leaders and managers is that leaders have people *follow* them, while managers have people who *work for* them…
> A successful business owner needs to be both a strong leader and manager to get their team on board to follow them towards their vision of success.[27]

It's expected that people in leadership positions (by which we mean those who sit at the top of the business food chain) can do both leadership and management seamlessly. But just because they're expected to be able to do both doesn't mean they can.

When one skill is missing, or both, bad things happen.

- Without a strategy, the business doesn't know *where* it's going.

- Without leadership, employees don't know *why* they're going there.
- Without management, no-one knows *how* to get there.

True leadership of the inspirational kind is difficult to define, really. It's more of a 'feeling' than a set of distinctive character sets. But one certainly knows when it's present and, by extension, when it's absent.

True leaders are realistic, but inspirational; set a direction and make people want to get on board; and can make their followers inexplicably sad when they're no longer around.

A lot of this comes down to charisma. David Taylor, author of *The Naked Leader*,[28] says that

> Charisma is a key component of true leadership. Every organisation has an enormous, latent force waiting to be released. Management will keep it stifled. Naked Leadership will set it free. And when it is free, everything else falls into place, automatically.
>
> When you meet someone charismatic you will feel inspired, yes. You will also feel warm, but above all you will feel your life has been touched by another. This is a feeling that is difficult to describe. The only word I can think of is magic.

I worked at one company where the CEO was charismatic, but dismally poor at creating a vision or encouraging people to get on board with that vision. The company didn't last. I worked at another company where the CEO was aggressive, argumentative and stubborn. The company muddled on, year after year, and the employees got increasingly miserable, year after year. Eventually, the profitable arm of the business was purchased by someone else – who saw its potential and, by changing things, increased revenues (and profits) exponentially.

I also worked at one where the CEO was the kind of person who remembered people's names, stood up on stage and commanded an audience, and inspired thousands of people to want to come to work every day. The company thrived and prospered.

I even worked at another where, when the true leader[j] left, the rest of his employees slowly but surely left too. As a result, the company couldn't turn a profit, and eventually had to downsize. His departure had a measurable impact on the company but, arguably more importantly, it forced the people who worked for him to confront their own leadership abilities, or lack thereof.

WHAT HAPPENS WHEN LEADERS LEAVE?

Have you ever worked for a real leader? At some point in time, if you're fortunate enough, you will have worked with or for a real leader. I specify the word 'real' because I solemnly believe that leaders are born, not made.

Don't get me wrong. People with innate talent for leadership can develop it – even if they don't realise they have it. And people can certainly be taught to act like leaders. But what I'm talking about is that 'spark', that indefinable 'something' that makes you feel like somehow you are *more* when you're with that person, and that together you are more than the sum of your parts. They can make you feel like you want to make them proud and, as a consequence, you do.

Great leaders will take their teams through adversity and out the other side. Great leaders will make people see that there's a better way, and help them have the courage in themselves to find that way, pursue it and reach it. But leaders are, after all, only human. And sometimes they move on – to lead other people.

So, what happens when leaders choose a different path?

When leaders leave, two things can happen: they can leave bits of themselves behind – their legacy – or they can leave a real hole in the hearts of the people who have been following them.

---

[j] Note: he was not the actual leader, i.e. the CEO – but another C-level executive, as well as being a leader who inspired others, who others trusted, and who gave people a sense of purpose and the desire to deliver on that purpose.

A while ago, a leader who inspired me enormously – someone who gave me permission to see myself as something more than I was, someone who gave me the courage to see my own ability to lead others – announced that he was leaving.

And a little bit of my heart broke.

The thing about broken hearts, though – and the thing about coping with the departure of someone you trust, respect and enjoy working with – is that it isn't really about *them*. It's about *you*. And it's a kind of 'death'. It's the death of 'the way things were'. And it takes a bit of time to get to grips with.

But there are two ways of dealing with that grief: you can mourn, get angry and depressed – and never leave that phase; or you can accept it and move on.

A good leader will help you work through that process, keep the lines of communication open and be there as much as they can during the transition time. If they have the opportunity, a good leader should have already prepared their staff for their departure (and potentially even put succession planning in place well in advance). But sooner or later, it's time to let them go.

Only then will those under their command find a way of coping with their loss. It might be to elect a new leader, to create co-leadership or to disband entirely. But if disbanding is not an option, the only choice is for employees to take their future into our own hands.

When leaders leave, it's time for other leaders to step into the breach. Only then will the future of an organisation, a team or a business be secure. And that, in its own way, is the sign of a good leader – because they inspire people enough to lead themselves.

The leader who left had me believing I was more than I was. He was unquestionably a leader, not only in the sense that he inspired others to get the job done, but also in the sense that he inspired others to become leaders in their own rights.

Which brings us to the core of this chapter.

LESSON 3: Your Secret Army can be supported or destroyed by your generals (managers and leaders).

Extracts of Sun Tzu's *The Art of War* find their way into management texts so often that when I finally read the full text, I was surprised to find that it was actually written as nothing more than a military hand guide. It surprised me because his simple – almost simplistic – lessons have been extrapolated to business strategy in such diverse and applicable ways.

In essence, Sun Tzu covers, amongst other areas: attack, strategy, alliances, army and cities. The modern equivalents of which differ only in that your 'army' is metaphorical and the 'cities' are your target market and your business locations. The book also covers the essential elements for victory, as quoted below:[29]

> Thus we may know that there are five essentials for victory:
> 1. He will win who knows when to fight and when not to fight.
> 2. He will win who knows how to handle both superior and inferior forces.
> 3. He will win whose army is animated by the same spirit throughout all its ranks.
> 4. He will win who, prepared himself, waits to take the enemy unprepared.
> 5. He will win who has military capacity and is not interfered with by the sovereign.

The point I wish to focus on here is 'He will win whose army is animated by the same spirit throughout its ranks.'

Charismatic leaders inspire that spirit, but they can't do it all on their own. They need people to plan, build, execute and deliver results. Leaders need managers (generals) to use that spirit in order to inspire the rest of the business (the ranks) to achieve the company's objectives (victory).

When managers and leaders need to motivate their ranks (employees) to meet company objectives, they need to know the answers to these two questions:

- Where is our company headed?
- Where do we (the managers) and our teams fit in?

We really *do* need to know this. Trust me. It's important. When people don't know where they're going, chaos ensues. People pull in different directions. They work at cross purposes. They think they're making progress, only to realise the progress is in the wrong direction. But they can't find the right direction on their own. They need leaders to inspire that direction, managers to keep them on the path, and something else to get them from good to great. This requires a different type of leadership altogether – someone who isn't just charismatic, but focused, determined and practical.

A foundational book on the art of strategy and leadership, *Good to Great* identifies consistently high-performing companies and what makes them special.[30] One of these ingredients is a special type of leader who knows that getting to the end result isn't just about leadership: it's about hard work. In these companies, the leader – and the people she/he surrounds herself/himself with – go beyond defining greatness in some nebulous way; they anchor it in reality, focus and refine it, then create a strategy to achieve it. (See Chapter 7 for more about strategy and turning it into reality).

They chase a vision for greatness by being really practical about how to get there: not by ignoring the facts or the people, but by researching the facts, getting the right people on board (and keeping them there) and refining their path.

The point here is that leaders of all kinds, shapes and sizes are required to get a company up and running and then to take it to the next level. Sometimes the requirements facing a leader will change over time, so they have to evolve or leave for another role where their skills are more appropriate. Regardless, every business needs to have people with the vision, the strategy *and* the ability to get things done.

How they get things done, how they feel about getting things done, and how managers can inspire, manage or cajole people into *wanting* to do their jobs (in addition to leaders inspiring them) comes down to strategy, planning and execution. Whether it works or not has a lot to do with whether people choose to treat their work as just a day job or see their work as meaningful. This has a lot to do with inspiration, and has a big impact on happiness – which I will discuss in the next chapter.

Key Takeaways:

- *Leadership, or the lack thereof, can make or break the power of your Secret Army.*

- *Leaders will inspire you while they lead you. Great leaders will inspire you to become a leader yourself, even if they leave.*

- *Your generals have a leadership responsibility, but they need to know where they're going – and so do their teams.*

Chapter 5: Your Power (The Secret of Happiness)

How can everyone in your business make themselves and the company better? It's all about being itchy… In this chapter, we talk about the concept of an itch and how to harness the power of being itchy. We discuss flow, what managers do, what great managers should do, and how putting the concept of flow into practice can help both individuals and businesses. We cover autonomy, mastery and purpose in more detail, introduce the concept of '20% time', talk about why happiness is everyone's own responsibility, and explain why we must stop defining ourselves using present participles.

What would you do if no-one paid you to do it? What's your compulsion, that thing that makes you passionate, that thing you would feel uncomfortable about – even itchy about – if you couldn't do it?

The 'itch' is that thing we can live without, if we have to, but if we do live without doing it we find that a piece of us is somehow lost. Something's missing. We are somehow diminished as a result of not having it in our lives.

I'm not talking about addiction here, like how a lot of people can't function without a cup of coffee first thing in the morning, or a cigarette (and, in my case, a cup of tea). I'm talking about the activities that keep a person sane.

For me, there are two itches in my life: writing and dancing.

I can go a few months without dancing, without moving in time to the ebb and flow of music and feeling the rhythm that takes over my body when I am perfectly in harmony. My muscles control the postures, my arms stretch and sway in time, my knees bend, my hips move from side to side, or glide, rotate, tilt or simply hold my body in space.

When I'm engaged in my 'itchy' activity, time stops. If I were in a darkened room, minutes or hours could pass and I would not know.

When I'm dancing, I'm in a state of what Mihaly Csikszentmihalyi calls 'flow', or optimal experience.[31] This is how he describes it: 'When a person invests all her psychic energy into an interaction… she in effect becomes part of a system of action greater than what the individual self had been before.' The way he describes it later in the book is that '[t]he flow experience, like everything else, is not "good" in an absolute sense. It is good only in that it has the potential to make life more rich, intense and meaningful; it is good because it increases the strength and complexity of the self.'

Flow happens in situations when people are challenged to perform at their best and are able to strive to achieve that best with no distractions. They are so focused on the task that nothing interrupts that 'perfect moment' until it's over, until they come back to reality with a bump and, hopefully, a feeling of utter exhilaration.

WHAT IF WE COULD DO THE THINGS THAT INSPIRE US?

I don't dance for a living. I don't even do it every week. But what if I could? What if I could do the thing I most love in the world every day of my life? Would I still love it if, in twenty or thirty years' time, I was still doing it? Would I still love it if I had to do it for a living, if my income and my family's well-being depended my ability to earn money from me indulging in my passion?

The sad fact is that the need to earn money from a hobby, even a passion, can often diminish the joy in that passion. Partly because, when we *have to* do something, we can often lose the will to do it. It becomes a task, a chore. That's partly why I don't dance for a living.

But what if we could indulge our passions in a way that made us challenged, yet enthused? And what if we could turn our lives into a search for the optimal flow experience – not just in our private lives, but also at work?

How can individuals and businesses 'harness the itch'?

This is a challenge for individuals and businesses alike – to identify how we can do two things:

- find out how to 'flow' in our work lives – to find that optimal state of performance, and

- find out what our 'purpose' is and be given the autonomy to continuously strive towards that purpose, so that we become more than people who just get things done, but, instead, do things because we believe in what we're doing and love doing it.

This is the true challenge of anyone in command of an army: to motivate his/her troops to achieve victory. It's the same challenge for the leader or manager of any company, or the leader of any team within a company.

There's a huge amount of responsibility on managers' shoulders.

So, what is the actual role of a manager? According to one of the classic management books that every first-year management student is required to study, analyse and regurgitate – Hellriegel & Slocum's textbook, *Management*[32] – '[a] manager is a person who allocates human and material resources and directs the operations of a department of an entire organisation.' What managers really do is a combination of these seven factors:[33]

- manage individual performance,
- instruct subordinates,
- plan and allocate resources,
- coordinate groups,
- manage group/department performance,
- monitor the business environment, and
- represent their team.

At least, that's what they did in 1989. Arguably, the fundamentals of management haven't changed much over time, but what has changed is the sheer volume of literature available about what differentiates a merely 'good' manager, from a 'great' manager.

If great companies know why they are in business in the first place (this isn't *just* about earning money); hire the right people (and aim to keep them on board); refine the *path* to greatness with the brutal facts of reality; and keep their people focused and motivated, even when times are tough, then their managers have to learn, embrace and execute a whole new set of skills.

A *Forbes* article by Victor Lipman says that these are the '5 Things the Best Managers Do and Don't Do':[34]

- keep the big picture in mind,
- be consistent in their behaviour,
- treat their employees' time as if it's as important as their own,
- be unafraid to question their own management, and
- earn the trust of those they manage.

Which leads us to the lesson of this chapter.

> **LESSON 4:** Your generals need to have people's hearts in mind.

When I was working for a non-profit organisation, I spent a lot of time – 30-50 minutes a day, possibly more – speaking with my manager about non-work-related things: his family, his ambitions, my plans, and what we were doing over the weekend. During those times, I never felt that he was in a rush, or impatient to get on with the next chore. On the contrary, I felt that it was important bonding time, time that allowed us to continue to work together effectively. And we did. Together we achieved extraordinary things – we managed to cut the costs of some products by up to 75 per cent, we built and improved databases and websites (back in the days when this was still a relatively new and exciting thing to achieve), we nurtured relationships with our contractors, and we used the feedback our contractors received from our customers to make further improvements. We did good work.

In other profit-focused businesses, these nearly hour-long daily conversations may be seen as a complete waste of time. However, they were anything but that! The time we spent processing our lives gave us several things:

- time to reflect – which often, but not always, inspired us to do things in our work lives in slightly different or better ways,

- a feeling of solidarity, and a sense that I had his back and he had mine, and
- the opportunity to say 'well done' to each other, and to express our concerns or frustrations about things going on in both our work and personal lives.

I'll never forget the impression this manager made on me. In fact, he was such an inspiration that I worked with him twice. Arguably, I must have been an inspiration to him too, because the first time I worked with him, I was actually just a temporary worker for a few months. I hardly expected him to remember me when I applied for a job with the same organisation several years later. It turns out, I discovered once I actually *had* the job, that the moment he saw my CV again, he decided he had to have me on board.

He's not the only manager I've worked with who understood the importance of bonding and sharing time. A line manager who regularly scheduled social events for our team (inside and outside of office hours) would do the same. When the time came to have our regular one-to-one meetings, she took care to make sure I knew that the time we spent together wasn't just for reporting on workloads and raising issues; it was time for us to spend together to talk about anything and everything we needed to discuss. These discussions were often personal, and could lead to helpful coaching sessions, but they also allowed us to talk about issues in the business that we might resolve by putting our heads together. They gave us the freedom to speak confidentially about problems and possibilities, people and personalities, ideas and initiatives.

She inspired me to do the same for my direct reports, and I found that the time I spent with my employees was beneficial for me too, both at the time and, upon reflection, in later life as well.

WORKPLACE BONDING AND HAPPINESS

I am a firm believer in the importance of bonding at work, whether in one-to-one meetings or in the kitchen (see

Chapter 14 for more about bonding in the kitchen). This 'non-work work time' has a role to play far beyond that of taking a break or making sure we don't get dehydrated. The social implications of those simple exchanges can actually have far-reaching consequences.

It's almost impossible to predict the powerful potential outcomes of sharing a cup of coffee, and a piece of your life, with a co-worker during those 'non-work work times', because they can be surprisingly long-term and far-reaching. For me, it has resulted in new work, continued friendships, and numerous ideas and workplace improvements, to name just a few benefits. It also has the potential to make people happier, generally. Sharing frustrations over a cup of tea has frequently given me the break, and the perspective, I needed to carry on working with a spring in my step. I'm willing to bet it's done the same for people with whom I've shared a moment of enthusiasm or a listening ear.

Mihaly Csikszentmihalyi spent twenty-five years studying the science of human happiness and, in the end, wrote a book called *Flow: The Psychology of Optimal Experience*.[35] He wasn't talking about taking coffee breaks in this extract from his book, but he could have been…

> What I 'discovered' was that happiness is not something that just happens.
>
> It is not the result of good fortune or random chance. It is not something that money can buy or power command. It does not depend on outside events, but, rather, on how we interpret them.
>
> Happiness, in fact, is a condition that must be prepared for, cultivated, and defended privately by each person. People who learn to control inner experience will be able to determine the quality of their lives, which is as close as any of us can come to being happy.

Whether we're choosing to change our perspective over a cup of java and a chat, or in some more lasting and esoteric way, it all comes down to finding those moments of delight, every day.

Drinking coffee is not likely to help us get into that brilliant zone of flow – but it offers us a momentary insight into how to find happiness every day at work in small ways.

The other thing having 'bonding time' with a line manager or direct reports does is identify opportunities to take on tasks that really *do* make us excited. When we are given the opportunity and encouragement, these tasks have the potential to 'scratch our itches' and put us into the moment of flow.

To return to Mihaly Csikszentmihalyi,[36] his research revealed a surprising commonality about what people experienced when they were truly happy in that moment of flow.

- The experience usually occurs when we confront tasks we have a chance of completing.
- We must be able to concentrate on what we are doing.
- The concentration is usually possible because the task undertaken has clear goals.
- The task provides immediate feedback.
- One acts with a deep but effortless involvement that removes from awareness the worries and frustrations of everyday life.
- Enjoyable experiences allow people to exercise a sense of control over their actions.
- Concern for the self disappears, yet paradoxically, the sense of self emerges stronger after the flow experience is over.
- The sense of duration of time is altered.

When people are involved in a task or activity they love, they enter this state of flow. In our private lives, we often get to enjoy these moments of flow – when we're with friends and time seems to have disappeared. For example, when we get to the end of a weekend and don't know where the time went – these are most likely to have been times of flow. We also experience this sense of flow when we're engaged in an activity that makes us come alive – the itch referred to earlier.

It is often incredibly difficult for many people to identify what their itch is. It's even harder to give ourselves permission to do that thing we're passionate about (which we'll cover next).

But the real magic happens when businesses are able to identify what people are passionate about and help them work towards that passion within the business. It helps people, and it helps the bottom line.

This is where your company's generals need to know what's in their troops' hearts, give them a reason to want to work towards that, and help them achieve what makes them passionate. Because no-one should have to go through life feeling 'itchy' all the time.

AUTONOMY, MASTERY AND PURPOSE

As mentioned in Chapter 2, Daniel Pink is the author of the best-selling book, *Drive: The Surprising Truth About What Motivates Us*.[37] Pink's book is hailed as transformational, but really, it's just good business practice. Great companies know that using the principles of autonomy, mastery and purpose embodied in his work is a matter of necessity.

Autonomy is the ability to have control over the tasks we do. Having mastery over an area of interest is about becoming better at something that matters (learning to be a master of your art). Purpose is arguably the biggest missing ingredient in modern companies. Humans inherently know that life is about (or, arguably, should be) more than just plodding through from day to day. We're looking for something that gets us up in the morning and makes us go to bed at night with a sense of satisfaction.

Companies who don't have a strong reason to exist are not helping their employees unless their employees can help themselves.

MY FIRST FULL-TIME JOB: SETTING UP AN INSTITUTE

I was fortunate enough, in my very first full-time job, to have all three of these elements. But I didn't know it at the time.

Setting up an institute may sound like a daunting task. Perhaps, in some ways, it was, but it didn't seem like it to me. I was tasked with turning a conceptual idea into a functioning organisation. When I started, we had funding and a building – that was all. Even the building wasn't available to move into immediately, as I discovered when I started the job and was housed in a tin-roofed annex across the campus – not a pleasant experience when the summer temperature regularly soared to 42 degrees centigrade!

I knew what I had to do, though: sort out furniture, equipment and even window blinds; get a finance system organised; set up marketing initiatives; support the business by running courses and making sure everything happened on time, in a comfortable location.

I was given the autonomy to make my own decisions about small, but interesting things: what kinds of chairs to purchase; what colour scheme to use; which printer type to buy, and so-on. I was allowed to master the skill of managing our finances. And I had a purpose: to create an organisation where students would want to come and learn, where they felt comfortable doing so, and where they had all the resources available at their disposal to learn effectively.

I wasn't left on my own to make the really hard decisions, nor was I abandoned to learn how to do organisation-specific tasks like figuring out ledger codes and accounting practices. Additionally, there was a clear sense of what needed to be done, and I had the skills and resources to do it.

It was all done in time, under budget, and then I got bored. They had given me autonomy, mastery and purpose to set up the organisation, so I sought the same elements in the rest of my work. Once I had their marketing up and running, they let me train people, and then they let me do my Master's degree part-time while I was running the organisation. Whenever I ran out of tasks to 'master', I sought more autonomy – and they gave it to me.

In retrospect, the autonomy, mastery and purpose I was given at this organisation set up the high expectations I've had of jobs ever since. In a way, it spoiled me – because it made me think that I *would* gain this kind of autonomy, mastery and purpose in all my jobs – and it made me believe that I *should.*

Over the years, I have learned that I'm not alone in having these high expectations – many of today's employees have them, particularly millennials and Gen-X. We expect more from our companies, possibly because many of us are taught, from an early age, that we can achieve great things and that we *should* do so. However, great companies know how to help us find *more* – more meaning in our work, more purpose, more control, and so-on.

But there are great examples of how companies are helping individuals find autonomy, mastery and purpose in the real world. I return to Daniel Pink's book to elaborate.

Autonomy

One of Pink's ideas is the concept of '20% time'. The idea is simple: let your employees spend one day a week (20 per cent of their time) on any problem they want. It worked for 3M – in fact, that's where the Post-it note came from. It worked for Google (we got Gmail, Google News, Google Sky and Google Translate from it), and the chances are that it might work for you. It's a strange and scary concept, but it's all about finding the flow by doing something that truly motivates and inspires you. The results will be beneficial for both the individuals and the business.

For businesses, the lesson is this: if 20 per cent seems unrealistic, it's possible to have smaller doses – say one afternoon a week – but it doesn't hurt to test it out for a few weeks and see if it helps. A word of warning, though: choose a time when individuals are most likely to be at their creative peak – or let them choose the time. Or, if giving employees time off to pursue interesting goals isn't a realistic possibility for your company, allow them to find better ways of working within their current roles. Doing this worked brilliantly for Paul O'Neill, the CEO of Alcoa (the Aluminum Company of America). We'll go into this story in a bit more detail in Chapter 10.

Mastery

Pink suggests that, instead of being motivated by extrinsic rewards, having a desire to 'do better' is what really drives success. He calls it 'Type I behaviour'. Simply, it means that if we live and work in a way that allows us to focus on producing meaningful results, it leads to 'stronger performance, greater health, and higher overall well-being'.[38]

So how do we find the opportunity to constantly improve at our jobs, to find mastery over our tasks? The answer lies in something called Goldilocks tasks. These are tasks that hit the sweet spot –they are 'neither too easy, nor too hard'.[39] When used in addition to regular, less inspiring tasks, Goldilocks tasks can help inspire flow, create a sense of pride and provide a challenge that will help us get, and remain, inspired.

For businesses, here's the lesson: finding Goldilocks tasks can be simpler than we think. If we give our employees the permission and autonomy to find tasks within their role at which they want to become a master, they will often choose Goldilocks tasks themselves. Alternatively, it's possible to turn normal tasks into Goldilocks tasks by varying the deadlines.

I had one challenging employee who did far better when he was able to select his own deadlines. Ironically, when he chose his own deadlines, they were often sooner than they would have been if I had chosen them. But he needed that pressure in order to turn boring tasks into Goldilocks ones.

Purpose

This might be the hardest of the three to turn into reality in most organisations, because many employees' purpose is largely determined by the company for which they work, particularly if they are perceived to be a small cog in a big machine. However, even if employees can't always find, or don't see, that the organisation exists to serve a deeper meaning or purpose, they can try and find purpose in their team, or in their work.

For me, it was easy to find purpose when I was working in that non-profit organisation – our job was, literally, to improve people's lives. It has been, arguably, harder to find purpose when working for organisations that don't have a stated goal of wanting to improve the world. Along the way, though, I learned an important lesson: 'making a difference' in someone's life doesn't have to mean that you're helping them change the world. Sometimes it's enough to know that you, or your company, or your product or service, is helping change individuals' lives in small ways, every day.

HAPPINESS IS EVERYONE'S RESPONSIBILITY

> The mass of men lead lives of quiet desperation.
>
> – Henry David Thoreau

As we go through this book and discuss the key elements of finding, supporting and leading your Secret Army to success, there is a risk that some will think it's entirely up to the army's leaders and generals to drive success.

It's not.

Happiness is everyone's responsibility. No-one can make their employees happy, and certainly not all the time. Companies, leaders and managers can create the conditions for employees to become happy – but it's up to the employees themselves to find the opportunities for happiness, and seize them.

If we're lucky, we might be able to work with others who demonstrate these *8 Signs an Employee is Exceptional (Which Never Appear on Performance Evaluations)*.[40]

1. They think well beyond job descriptions.
2. They're quirky…
3. And they know when to rein in their individuality.
4. They praise other people in public…
5. And they disagree in private.
6. They ask questions when others won't.
7. They like to prove other people wrong.
8. They're constantly exploring.

These are signs of self-motivated people who are striving for something more. It's something many of us often aim to do – but some just don't know *how*, or *don't have the confidence*, to do these things.

But here's a newsflash.

No-one is going to give us 'permission' to take control of our lives. They're just not.

It's all very well to build a life plan – if we actually know what we want in the first place – but that does not help one iota if we're going to spend our whole lives waiting for 'the right time' or 'the right place' to get started. It's like sitting at a bus stop, waiting for a bus that will never arrive, or on a bench waiting for a friend who you've forgotten to make an appointment with.

So how do we get started? We've all heard inspirational quotes like 'Winners never quit, quitters never win' etc. etc. They're true, of course, but what if we're not naturally one of the world's winners? Or, if we have a winning strategy, idea or embryonic passion inside, but are *too afraid to get started*.

Here's the good news: if you feel like this you are not alone.

The population of people who spend their life do*'ing'* something, and never getting it done, is innumerable! Think about it – I'm willing to bet you could name at least half a dozen people who are living their life in the present continuous tense, in the moment of *'ing'*.

'I'm writ*ing* a book.'
'I'm work*ing* on my thesis.'
'I'm find*ing* myself.'

None of these are bad things on their own. In fact, they're great – as long as they are a means to an end. But there is a risk – and it's not just a small one – that people who spend too long *talking* about be*ing* or do*ing* never actually get it done! Instead, they find themselves living in a state of perpetual incompletion. Their identity actually becomes associated with never finishing the thing itself.

I have some experience with waiting for permission to get something done.

For years I was writing a romantic fiction novel. Note the present participle: writ*ing*. But it was only once I *stopped being afraid* of finishing a novel that might have turned out to be fantastic, or terrible, that I actually got it done. I was waiting for someone to give me permission to finish it – for permission to deliver a piece of work that would not be perfect. I waited a long, long time.

Then something changed: I committed to a deadline, for myself. I gave myself permission to finish writing it – no matter how good or bad it ended up being.

That is one of the few reasons I have written a novel (in addition to the non-fiction book you're reading now) and I am no longer writing one. I may not have published it yet, but at least I'm not living in a perpetual state of setting myself a goal that I may never deliver on, and disappointing myself in the process. It's done. I can move on with life.

DON'T DEFINE YOURSELF IN THE CONTINUOUS PRESENT

Unfortunately, there are many novelists – and doubtless, many other people with varied and interesting goals – who define themselves in the continuous present. They are writers precisely because they *are* writing a novel: always writing, never *'finished writing'*, never *'have written'*.

There is a huge risk that if we spend so much of our lives being too afraid to finish something, to commit to getting the job done – no matter how good or bad that job might be – we end up in a perpetual never-never land. Never finished, never quite confident enough to get to an end product.

Well, the thing is, no-one is ever going to give us permission to finish our thing, whatever it is. That's entirely up to us. We need to give ourselves permission.

The same applies at work. Do you have a great idea? I'm sorry to be the bearer of hard-to-hear news, but, as a wise colleague of mine, Melissa Romo, was told at the beginning of her career, 'It's not a thing until it's a thing.' When saying these words her mentor meant, as far as I can gather, 'Go ahead, have the ideas, but please, please, don't stop there!'

I can picture her mentor saying something like this: 'Don't stop with the idea. I'm not going to tell you that it's okay to create an idea or apply it to improve your business. That's not for me to say. It's for you to produce. It's your responsibility to take that idea and apply it.'

Give *yourself* permission to do something you're afraid of.

So, here's something to try today: give yourself permission to do something you're afraid of, reluctant to attempt or reluctant to finish. Don't wait until it's perfect. Just get it done. And then put it 'out there' in whatever format it takes. Maybe no-one will like it or appreciate it, but at least it will be done. And then you can stop seeing yourself in the present continuous.

Here's the formula of 'ing' – insert appropriate words:

Stop being a Y (insert noun here) because you're Y-*ing* (insert present participle), be a Y (noun) because you have Y-*ed/en* (past participle). For example, stop being a writer because you're writing. Be a writer because you have written. Stop being a leader because you're trying to lead. Be a leader because you have led.

And then be proud of the fact that you've been brave enough to turn your vision into reality.

No one else is going to give us permission. It's up to us to give ourselves permission to get it done.

WHAT REALLY MAKES A SECRET ARMY POWERFUL?

To conclude this section of the book, let me summarise it this way: money makes the world go round, but people make it worth living in.

So far, we've covered lessons about the value of our employees, our customers and our managers. But, ultimately, any individual's success comes down to their ability and willingness to do something passionately, diligently, with focus or for a purpose. The secret of the Secret Army lies in combining all the forces and resources available at its disposal and turn them towards a single goal: the defeat of another army in a meaningful war.

What's your war? How important is it to win the war? And how do you get people to march those dreary weeks alongside you in your quest? That's what the next section, 'Are you leading forwards or sideways?' is all about.

Key Takeaways:

- *The success or failure of an army lies in its ability to meet its objectives. It may seem naïve to believe that happiness is critical to success but, if your army's functionality depends on its ability to work well, then happiness is a major element. Yet, happiness is everyone's responsibility. Companies, leaders and managers can create the conditions for employees to be happy – but it's up to employees themselves to find the opportunities for happiness and seize them.*

- *No-one is going to give us 'permission' to take control of our lives. It's all very well to build a life plan, but that doesn't help one iota if we're going to spend our whole lives waiting for 'the right time' or 'the right place' to get started.*

- *Stop being a Y (insert noun here) because you're Y-ing (insert present participle), be a Y (noun) because you have Y-ed/en (past participle).*

SECTION 2

ARE YOU LEADING FORWARDS OR SIDEWAYS?

Chapter 6: Who Are You Anyway?

What do trees, drama, 5 Whys, Essentialism and The Secret Army have in common? This chapter will explain all this using the concept of 'simplify and amplify', the 5 Whys, and the importance of prioritisation. We cover the need to achieve, and why it's important for businesses to understand the essence of what they do, and explain it to their employees.

SIMPLIFY AND AMPLIFY

At university I had a drama lecturer I didn't really get on with. She was driven and driving – but we saw the world from different perspectives. I wanted to perform, she wanted to analyse. I wanted to feel beautiful on stage, she wanted to be meaningful on stage. I wanted to delight an audience, she wanted to challenge them. I was young, she was less so.

I resented her feedback on my research project at the time. I had great ideas, super execution, passion, creativity, fire, and the ability to engage and enthuse people. I thought that was enough. She realised it wasn't. But we were both headstrong and so, while I learned some valuable lessons from her, our relationship was fraught.

But there's one thing she taught me about drama that has stood me in good stead a long, long time later, and it all ends with a tree.

Studying drama at university could be argued to be a complete and utter waste of time. Drama students will disagree, of course, and to be fair, my drama school has turned out theatre producers who are in a league of their own and will be at least some of the famous names of their generation. So studying drama wasn't an entire waste – for them at least.

But for me, not only was it a bit of a waste of time (if I'm truly honest) – it was also incredibly frustrating. You see, my drama school didn't believe in simply studying and reproducing the classics, dancing beautifully and producing exquisite sets. For them, it was about challenging people's assumptions about theatre, making their brand of dance interesting (but frankly quite ugly, in my opinion), and producing low-budget sets that were 'interesting' more than realistic. I suppose that's what you get for going to a university where leaders learn, because leaders don't just accept the status quo: they challenge it.

So they challenged me and I, in my own way, challenged them right back.

I came to the department with a lifetime of dance training under my belt – ballet, modern, jazz, Spanish, tap, contemporary, ballroom and Latin American dancing – I could do them all. And I loved doing them. I loved the feeling of being on stage, of using the music to emphasise the beauty of the movement, the staccato stops, the lyrical flows, and the dramatic turns or falls or splits.

But they didn't want traditional dance, or the use of music in a traditional sense, for that matter. So, by third year, when it was too late to change my second major unless I wanted to repeat another two years of university (which I really did not want to do), I simply had to put up with this flagrant disregard for what I considered to be beautiful.

Our end of year project required us to create a piece of 'dance'. I use the inverted commas because while it was dance, it was not dance as you know it. Theoretically, it was based on contemporary dance or physical theatre. In reality, it was more like trying to throw yourself at the ground and miss. In my opinion, it was based on brutality, ugliness and an obsession with so-called 'meaning' in theatre. It wasn't like any dance I'd ever known.

This self-created piece had to be site-specific – by which they meant 'pick a location, choose what's meaningful about it, and perform with that in mind'. So I picked a tree. And I danced to music from Orff's *Carmina Burana*. For me, it was about celebrating the joy and life of a provocative, emotional piece of music and going back to everything I felt dance should stand for: beauty, movement, music, lyricism and talent.

Oh, what an arrogant little sod I was. Why on earth should I have been surprised when, after three years of the Drama Department trying to teach me to challenge the dynamics of dance, I wasn't awarded top marks when I simply followed the status quo (albeit amidst a huge pile of autumn leaves and the trees of the library quadrangle)? But I was.

In hindsight, it would have been possible to combine my passion for beauty and movement *with* meaning – the meaning of the location, the time of year, the people moving past, the environment, the context. But I wasn't really sure how to do it and, arguably more importantly, I was rebelling against the need to do what they were teaching me to do: to simplify and amplify 'dance' as I knew it.

Regardless of how ill-fated my tree dance was, my drama lecturer's words, 'simplify and amplify', have stuck with me to this day.

As I understand it, what she meant was this: strip it down to the barest elements. Find what makes it great. Go beyond that. Find what makes it remarkable. Go beyond that. Find what makes it 'essential'. And then take that, and amplify it – make it bigger, make it more, make it extraordinary.

To do that required a process of self-assessment that the department encouraged, but that wasn't always easy to embrace. Only many, many years later has it become evident to me that their process was more about questioning the status quo than reproducing it. They were trying to force us to ask 'Why?' more.

THE 5 WHYS

Have you ever wondered why kids ask 'Why?' almost incessantly when they're at that stage of development (around 3-4 years old)?[41] It's not just to drive parents crazy (although parents probably think it is). It's their way of trying to make sense of the world.[k] But it's not only children who benefit from asking 'Why?' again and again. There's actually a technique called the '5 Whys' that has been used with great success. The Toyota Motor Corporation developed it when they were

---

[k] An alternative theory by paediatrician, Dr Alan Green, is that 'Why?' doesn't actually mean 'How does it work'. It's simply their way of saying, 'That's interesting to me. Let's talk about that together. Tell me more, please?'

evolving how to manufacture cars better. Since then, it has been made famous through books like *The 7 Day Weekend* by Ricardo Semler, and it has been adopted as an element of the Six Sigma Project Management Methodology[42] to determine the root cause of an issue. 5 Whys is a technique that literally involves asking the same question multiple times. Here's how it works, according to SixSigmaonline.org:

> By repeatedly asking the question 'Why' (five is a good rule of thumb), you can peel away the layers of symptoms which can lead to the root cause of a problem. Very often the ostensible reason for a problem will lead you to another question. Although this technique is called '5 Whys,' you may find that you will need to ask the question fewer or more times than five before you find the issue related to a problem.[43]

This is a very helpful tool to do exactly what my drama lecturer advised: strip any task back to its essence. However, humans aren't usually particularly good at applying this to their lives.

Life is so busy that it's so easy to get distracted. To do things because they have to be done – or so many of us think. So those who do think like this end up with a thousand things that need to be done – many of them immediately – and no time to do them in. There's a reason Virtual PAs exist. There's a reason that dog-walkers, house-cleaners, lawn-mowing and garden maintenance people have jobs: they do tasks that cash-rich, time-poor people would rather outsource than tackle.

In fact, with organisations like TaskRabbit,[44] a London-based agency where you can hire resources (people) to do almost any job around the house– no matter how simple or complex – it just goes to show that an entire economy has been built around the fact that our lives are simply too busy – and too complex.

That's where someone like Greg McKeown comes in. He writes about why less often *really is* more. He calls it *Essentialism: The Disciplined Pursuit of Less.*[45] He says that

'Essentialism is not about how to get more things done; it's about how to get the *right* things done.'

If you don't prioritise your life, someone else will. He continues,

> The idea that we can have it all and do it all is not new… What *is* new is how especially damaging this myth is today, in a time when choice and expectations have increased exponentially. It results in stressed people trying to cram yet more activities into their already overscheduled lives. It creates corporate environments that talk about work/life balance but still expect their employees to be on their smartphones 24/7/365…
>
> In the same way that our wardrobe gets cluttered as clothes we never wear accumulate, so do our lives get cluttered as well-intentioned commitments and activities we've said yes to pile up. Most of these efforts didn't come with an expiry date. Unless we have a system for purging them, once adopted, they live on in perpetuity.[46]

Greg McKeown tells the story of writer, Nora Ephron, and her inspiration by a high school journalism teacher who taught her about the true 'essence' of a story – what makes a great lead or headline: the crux of the matter.

The teacher asked his students to come up with headlines about the fact that on Thursday next week all the high school teachers would be travelling to hear someone speak about new teaching methods. Students worked away at creating headlines. But they totally missed the point, until the teacher finally showed them: the headline needed to be based on the lead (i.e. the essence) that *there will be no school on Thursday!*

> 'In that instant', Ephron recalled, 'I realised that journalism was not about regurgitation of the facts, but about figuring out the point. It wasn't enough to know the who, what, when and where; you had to understand what it meant. And why it mattered.'

And that is what trees, drama, 5 Whys, Essentialism and The Secret Army have in common.

People need to understand what work means. And why it matters.

WHAT DOES SUCCESS MEAN TO YOU?

When I was rebelling against redefining dance, the biggest struggle for me was understanding why I had to reject what I loved about dancing in the first place. To me, success meant producing a great performance. As far as I can gather, to my lecturer, success meant producing a meaningful performance, a performance that would challenge people via dance and force them to ask questions. She wanted to redefine movement as 'thought' rather than 'beauty'.

I wasn't alone in this struggle at the time. Neither is anyone else who is struggling to figure out why they can't achieve what they desire – particularly if their motivation or understanding of why they do it is at odds with their manager's explanation of it, or their company's reasoning for doing it. Motivated employees are also driven to achieve something, and they're always driven *by* something too.

While some individuals can simply work towards an objective because they've been told to do it, others crave some kind of meaning in their work. If people struggle to wake up in the morning and drag themselves to the office or the plant or the site, and if they lead 'lives of quiet desperation', they clearly have an underlying need that's not being met.

In order to answer the question of what success means to their company and their employees, great companies have spent vast fortunes hiring consultants, management theories and brand experts. It is, unquestionably, not a simple task, but I believe it is critical.

What is even more important is for everyone working in a business to understand, collaboratively, what drives them – and to be honest when they're not driven by the same things.

Knowing the essence that underpins who we are and why we do things is the difference between a student droning on about a teacher's conference and knowing that the real story is there's no school. It's the difference between me dancing around a tree or creating a thought-provoking piece of art. It's about employees doing a day job or spending a day meaningfully, getting something out of it – and it starts by simplifying, and amplifying, everything.

> **LESSON 5:** Knowing why we do what we do makes fighting a war *worth fighting*. To keep your Secret Army fighting for your side, people need to understand what work means, and why it matters.

Key Takeaways:

- *What do trees, drama, 5 Whys, Essentialism and The Hidden Army have in common? People need to understand what doing an activity means to them; and why it matters.*

- *'Simplify and amplify' means that, whatever you do, in order to do it really well you must strip it down to the barest elements. Find what makes it remarkable. And then take that point and amplify it – make it bigger, make it more, make it extraordinary.*

- *Greg McKeown says, 'Essentialism is not about how to get more things done; it's about how to get the right things done.' If you don't prioritise your life, someone else will.*

- *Businesses must help their employees understand who they are and why they do things, in order to give meaning to their lives. It helps them, personally, and it makes good business sense in the long run.*

Chapter 7: Your Vision and Strategy

No war could be fought, or won, without strategy. But what is it, and why is it relevant? In this chapter, we talk about good and bad strategy, how to define a clear strategy, and the importance of addressing four strategic questions. We speak about vision too, and discuss how all these elements come together to develop strategic goals and enable leaders to empower their teams.

> When companies first start, leaders tend to be laser-focused on a clearly defined market opportunity. Originally, they develop a strategy that is simple and easy for everyone to understand. They ensure everyone on the team is aligned with the vision and mission; remind the team each day of the company's higher purpose; and make sure everyone is clear on how the company should be positioned in the market. They even make sure the corporate story they're sharing with customers is clear, compelling and consistent across all critical touch points.[1]

When companies first start, they know who their enemies are, and they implicitly understand the importance of their Secret Army in helping them win each battle. In other words, as Chris Zook and James Allen put it: 'successful businesses start off with a clear, insurgent mission on behalf of underserved customers. They are at war with their industry and each employee understands the company's bold vision and is inspired by it. Yet as a company grows over time, this insurgent mission and sense of purpose can become diluted'.[47]

VISION

It's easy to see when a company has a clear vision, and the benefits are felt across the organisation and beyond. Those

---

[1] Thanks to James O'Gara, CEO and Founder, OnMessage, for allowing me to use this extract from his brilliant 'OnMessage Minute' email entitled 'Every CEO and Founder Should Read This...'

companies that know what they're trying to achieve, and focus every element of their business on working towards a single, unifying purpose, are often business leaders in their field. Their vision is often encapsulated in the form of a mission statement that drives company philosophy and action (although not always).

A few notable examples of companies with great mission statements and clear visions include Microsoft, LinkedIn and Trip Advisor.[48]

When Microsoft first started, their mission was to put a personal computer on every desk. They succeeded, and then some. Today, their mission statement is 'To enable people and businesses throughout the world to realize their full potential' – the jury is out on whether they're achieving that or not, but their Surface Pro is certainly an innovation that allows them to head towards this lofty goal.

LinkedIn's mission statement is 'to connect the world's professionals and make them more productive and successful' – I'd say they're succeeding.

Trip Advisor says their mission is 'to help people around the world plan and have the perfect trip.'

These three companies, and many like them, have a guiding statement that goes beyond pretty words. It's actually enacted on a daily basis by their employees, and when done extraordinarily well, these statements help both employees and suppliers make decisions more easily. They align activities, they provide meaning and they define purpose.

VISION REQUIRES VISIONARIES – IT ALSO REQUIRES INFORMATION

Vision requires foresight. Indeed, the term 'vision' comes from the concept of seeing – seeing into the future, seeing beyond the ordinary. But it also consists of looking outwards, not inwards.

Vision has to start with visionaries – people who can see the world the way it should, or could, be. But it also requires the right information to determine the accuracy, or likelihood, of those visions becoming reality – otherwise it's just a dream.

Today, it is easier than ever before to find information that can lead to competitive advantage in support of a vision. Yet few are taking advantage of their vast quantities of data – mostly because turning data into insight is still a challenge.

According to DataScience, Inc.

> Forrester Consulting conducted a study which identified a minority of firms (22%) that were "Insights Leaders," companies that embed analytics and data science into their operating models to bring insights – actionable knowledge resulting from analytical models and algorithms – into every decision.[49]

They call these companies Insights Leaders, and these Insights Leaders use data science for competitive advantage. They tend to be small, agile disruptors (although they are not exclusively so). The point this article makes is that most firms miss the keys to good data science (i.e. insight) because they tend to *focus on the data*. In other words, they focus only on data collection, rather than on figuring out how to *turn that data into action*.

It's not enough to have a great vision. It has to be implemented. So, whose job is it, really, to provide vision within a business? Is it the company's senior leadership, or its middle management?

Some may believe that vision is the domain of our company's senior leaders. Yes, it certainly is. But it's also the job of the leaders in each individual business unit, segment or team, to give their group of subordinates – no matter how large or small – a sense of purpose.

How is it done? Step-by-step, brick-by-brick.

I am reminded of a story I've heard told in many different ways, by many different people, that has one key underlying theme: it's about perspective. This version comes from Jean Storlie:[50]

> A man came upon a construction site where three people were working. He asked the first, "What are you doing?" and the man replied: "I am laying

bricks." He asked the second, "What are you doing?" and the man replied: "I am building a wall." As he approached the third, he heard him humming a tune as he worked, and asked, "What are you doing?" The man stood, looked up at the sky, and smiled, "I am building a cathedral!"

No matter what role we play within an organisation, we can choose to believe that we are an important part of something bigger. Great leaders will help their teams do it instinctively. Others can learn to do it. But vision creates meaning that can go far beyond individual tasks or people.

STRATEGY

So if vision is a way of providing a sense of direction for a company, what is the role of strategy?

If you have ever been confused about the term strategy, you're forgiven.

The dictionary defines strategy as 'a plan of action designed to achieve a long-term or overall aim',[51] and this seems obvious enough but, according to the author of *Good Strategy, Bad Strategy*, Richard Rumelt,[52]

> The gap between good strategy and the jumble of things people label 'strategy' has grown over the years. But this plenitude has not brought clarity. Rather, the concept has been stretched to a gauzy thinness as pundits attach it to everything from utopian visions, to rules for matching your tie with your shirt.

Why is strategy so badly mislabelled? In part, because people think that any meaningful plan, designed to perform a specific outcome, can be labelled 'strategy'. But they're wrong (we're all wrong!).

Strategy isn't a way of thinking; it's a process.

Max McKeown[53] says, 'Strategy is about shaping the future.' He continues, 'There's no need for strategy definitions to be unclear or complicated.[m] Strategy is, essentially, knowing what the situation really is (knowing what you want and whether it will work or not), knowing what to do about it (how to achieve it), and doing it – but on a macro level. (We'll come back to this concept again in Chapter 13.)

Or, as he describes in *The Strategy Book*,[54] strategy enables a business to answer these questions.

- What do we want to do?
- What do we think is possible?
- What do we need to do to achieve our goals?
- When should we react to new opportunities and adapt plans?

Strategy can then be used as a guiding force that enables employees to take action.

Great strategy begins when leaders come together, use information to validate their intuition, and turn these insights into a plan – but that's only the beginning. Strategy is merely theoretical until it's interpreted, communicated and executed correctly.

Unfortunately, the devil is in the details. In some ways, perhaps, the very popularity (hence, over-use) of the word strategy may have led to its downfall – so says this quote from Forbes.[55]

> According to a recent Harvard Business Review article, "When CEOs Talk Strategy, Is Anyone Listening?" only a fraction of our workforce is really clued in…. even in high-performing companies with "clearly articulated public strategies," only 29% of their employees can correctly identify their company's strategy out of six choices… That means 70% (7 out of 10) of all employees (yes, even yours) are unknowingly misaligned with your company's strategic direction.

---

[m] This clarification comes from personal discussions with Max, who kindly elaborated on this point via email.

It's almost enough to make one give up hope.

And yet, there is still a reason for someone in the organisation to be responsible for caring deeply about strategy and its execution – someone who wakes up every day and asks this critical question: 'What are we currently doing to ensure every employee knows where we are going and what they should be doing to help us get there.' Why? Because, according to McKinsey and Company, 'When people understand and are excited about the direction their company is taking, the company's earnings margin is twice as likely to be above the median.'[56]

WHEN GOOD STRATEGY WORKS

But just like strategy, all of this is just theory until it's turned into reality. So, here's an example of how good strategy can become great reality.

We return to the story of Concur. In Chapter 1 we used the founders of Concur as an example of good leadership. Certainly, that's what lead to their exponential growth and their powerful workforce. But it's also worth telling the story of how they transformed their travel and expenses business from being focused on big business to one that could be bought and used by small- and medium-sized enterprises and, as a result, became an indomitable force in the industry.

We've heard how Steve, Raj and Mike created Concur. However, these clever guys knew that if they could build a business from scratch – so could others. The way I heard this story told,[n] they were terrified that two clever people from MIT were going to sit somewhere and build an expenses product that was almost as good as Concur and give it to small companies – for free.

So, initially, Steve, Raj and Mike's entire SME strategy started as a defensive one.

Their goal was to enable SMEs to take advantage of technology and simplify their internal processes without the

---

[n] My thanks go to James Wilkinson for telling this story in his own words, as he lived through it when he was working at Concur.

burden of costs or resources being too high. They asked themselves, 'How do we build something that little companies can afford?', and then they challenged their best employees to do just that. Concur spent a year with selected research and development, implementation and marketing teams. Their goal was to create 'the art of the possible'.

They did it by automating the software setup so that businesses didn't have to pay as much for every software implementation. To do it, they had to create prescriptive software and simplify the implementation. Once they figured out how to do this, they were able to reduce the heavy cost overheads and bring the benefits of an automated process to the SME market.

They did it. Then they had to sell it.

In the early days, people wouldn't buy it, so they gave it away as a free trial. The market loved it, and once they were hooked, they were happy to pay a few hundred pounds a month. Job done.

They also discovered something amazing. Where previously they had assumed that everyone wanted a bespoke version of the software, they discovered that most people were enjoying getting a 'best-practice' version with a prescribed process, along with the ability to change configurations within the programme without a programmer needing to sit down to write more code.

Ultimately, Concur created a specialist arm of their business to deal with the SME market. This market became one of their two core business groups: each with completely different strategic aims.

With this new product, the result was increased market share and, ultimately, a very lucrative offer from SAP which was, simply, too good to turn down. They still have competitors, certainly, but they are market leaders.

WHEN STRATEGY GOES BAD

In contrast, if you want to know about bad strategy, simply walk down to the end of your road and take a look at the empty store. Their name might still be above the door, in some cases.

And you may be able to spot an empty shelf, or one or two forlorn movie posters on the floor. Back in the day, many happy hours were spent browsing the shelves of Blockbuster video. Whatever happened to them?

Here's the story.

Blockbuster video could have bought Netflix for $50 million in the 1990s but, according to Dain Dunston,[57] 'when a boardroom dispute resulted in a change of CEO the new man didn't understand what business Blockbuster was really in. He started changing the game plan, including pulling out of their internet efforts.' Anecdotally, he decided there wasn't really a market in streaming because the internet wasn't fast enough. They failed to see future trends, didn't realise how attractive the convenience factor would become, and didn't see Netflix as a competitor.

We all know what happened next. It happened to Blockbuster, and it will happen to many, many companies in future. As Dunston put it, 'When a once successful company loses touch with the purpose that made it great, disaster follows.'[58]

Or, to quote the words of James O'Gara, CEO of OnMessage:[o]

> If you recognise that your business strategy has gotten cloudy and employees can no longer understand how they connect with the bigger picture; if your purpose, vision, mission and values are no longer actively embraced up and down the organisation; if words and actions from your leadership team no longer align with or support your corporate story and strategy; and if employees lack connection with, understanding of, or belief in your story and strategy, it's time to fix things. Fast.

---

[o] Thanks to James O'Gara, CEO and Founder, OnMessage, for allowing me to use this extract from his brilliant 'OnMessage Minute' email entitled 'Every CEO and Founder Should Read This...'

It is possible to regain that clarity and alignment, but it requires commitment from you, your leaders, and your middle management teams. And it requires intentional, concerted effort and energy – up and down the organisation.

FOCUS

Good strategy also requires focus.

We live in a VUCA world[59] – a world of Volatility, Uncertainty, Complexity and Ambiguity. Consequentially, it's all too easy to lose focus. So, as Richard Rumelt[60] puts it, 'Good strategy requires leaders who are willing and able to say *no* to a variety of actions and interests.' Unfortunately, according to him, 'Many bad strategies are just statements of desire rather than plans for overcoming obstacles.'[61]

It is, of course, good (nay, essential) to have a statement of desire. It gives people focus and direction. But this statement should come *as a result of* having considered all the options and then putting plans in place to make things happen, to solve problems along the way and to reach that end goal.

The best strategies don't need to be complex. Indeed, some of the best strategies can be extraordinarily simply described, and simple (not *easy*!) to execute. It's their focused simplicity that makes them great – precisely because they don't do 'fluff', or what Rumelt calls 'a form of gibberish masquerading as strategic concepts or arguments.'[62]

Fluff helps no-one, and fluffy strategies do more harm than good. Delete the fluff!

Strategies have to be clear, but also have to be communicated and executed well. Even the best strategy in the world will fail if it's isolated from the real world and the real activities of your business, your team members or what they're trying to do day-to-day.

Strategy is often thought to be the domain of C-level leadership – and it should be – but it shouldn't be created by C-level execs in isolation. Nor should strategy only be available to those at the top. As we discuss later, in the chapter on *Undiscovered Idea-Generators*, ideas can come from surprising sources. Ignoring great ideas from employees can work to the detriment of the business.

Indeed, when idea-generation is truly welcomed across the company, it can form an important part of a truly broad-thinking business strategy. As Max McKeown puts it, [63]

> Strategy is not really a solo sport – even if you're the CEO. At its most effective, it involves people and knowledge at all levels, inside and outside the organisation... Ideally, the strategy process should engage the hearts and minds of the whole company continually throughout the year. The strategy is the company, and the company is the strategy. It follows that imaginative and knowledgeable involvement with a fluid, dynamic strategy process is helpful.

His recommendation is to 'co-create a strategy model debated by your organisation',[64] and 'simplify the strategy into a model that makes sense to everyone', the reason being that 'if it has been created with them then it has meaning, so they are emotionally engaged with *their* strategy for winning'.

This, really, is the essence of the argument this book puts forward: involve people, engage them, listen to them, empower them, keep them focused, give them opportunities to grow, and give them challenges. The result is better business.

> **LESSON 6:** Every army needs a strategy to win the war. Get strategic in a meaningful way by building a vision that is easy to execute and figuring out how to do it. Then delete the 'fluff' that distracts people.

Key Takeaways:

- *Clear vision is the guiding light of good strategy – but it's easy to lose this laser focus over time.*

- *Strategy is a process. It's merely theoretical until it's interpreted, communicated and executed correctly.*

- *We may believe that it is our company's job to provide a vision – and it is – but it's also the job of the leaders of each individual business unit, segment or team to give their cohort of the Secret Army – no matter how large or small – a sense of purpose.*

- *Strategy is the bedrock of action; but once strategy takes on a life of its own, it becomes a living, breathing thing that empowers people to take their own decisions. Then these decisions, in a beautiful circle of greatness, create real, focused actions. Ultimately, done right, strategy means that vision turns into reality.*

SECTION 3

THE SECRET
RESOURCES THAT
GREAT LEADERS USE

Chapter 8: Truth-tellers

Do we live in the era of authenticity? This chapter reveals how marketing can uncover the truth that excites your prospects, and helps them help themselves. We also talk about how to find the truth within your business; the roles of whingers and truth-tellers; and how to encourage truth-tellers to speak up.

MARKETING: TRUTH OR FICTION?[p]

When I got my first full-time job in 2003, I *didn't even know* what marketing was. But I had my suspicions, and they weren't good. I thought that all marketing was advertising and, by extension, lying. I hated lying and, therefore, I distrusted both marketing and advertising.

So I joined a non-profit, academic organisation that helps journalists – the very people who stand for truth – lead other journalists to find their own truths.

I didn't want to be a marketer/liar/advertiser when I set up their first website, wrote brochure copy and press releases and collected customer questionnaires.

Then it dawned on me... what I was doing wasn't advertising. It wasn't lying. But it *was* extremely clever, and extremely powerful. By creating messages that reach people who have a problem to solve, I realised that marketing can, cleverly and honestly, get into people's heads to actually help them help themselves. It helped me by luring me into a profession I now love. Marketing gave me what I secretly wanted, but didn't even know I wanted, and I realised its potential to help others too.

Leaders of great companies know that marketing is their ally.

It helps them give their customers what they want – either because their customers *do* know they want it or by helping people find a solution they may not have known existed.

---

[p] This content is based on a TEDx talk I gave called *Confessions of a liar: marketing in the era of authenticity.* TEDx Reading 2016. Retrieved 18 January 2017 from https://www.youtube.com/watch?v=FTJLbnq48nI

Thanks to the internet, and the democratisation of information, it's a great time to be a consumer. But it's an even better time to be a marketer, because right now, marketing and the bad smell that hung around the dishonesty of immoral advertising of yesteryear couldn't be farther from each other.

Today, I believe we live in the era of authenticity.

Our world is very different now to the heyday of television advertising in the 1950s – when it was the primary medium for influencing public opinion. Don't get me wrong, it wasn't all lies. But it certainly wasn't all true. In fact, even as relatively recently as 1979, the French advertiser Jacques Seguela wrote a book about advertising. It was called 'Don't tell my mother I work in advertising. She thinks I play piano in a brothel.'

Today, however, these advertisers of yesteryear would shudder to know that their carefully-woven fabrications can be unravelled at the drop of a hat – or the share of a tweet.

SO WHAT ARE THE IMPLICATIONS FOR COMPANIES?

Today, companies can't afford to lie. Never mind the fact that it's unethical, it's too easy to be found out, and it's definitely not profitable. Today, brands who lie simply won't survive. We've learned that from a variety of sources including (but not limited to) the Arab Spring and the BP oil spill.

Today, false tactics like Volkswagen's emissions scandal and Nurofen's misleading packaging can be exposed. It may be going too far to say that businesses who don't tell the truth will frankly, no longer have a business, but it's undeniable that, in our era of authenticity, the power lies with the consumer, not the advertiser.

Here are some statistics to prove this point.

Even though advertising is still extremely popular (in fact, according to the Internet Advertising Bureau UK, British advertisers spent nearly £4 billion on digital advertising in the first half of 2015 – that's up 13.4 per cent year on year), consumers have had enough of messages being shoved at them. People are actually *paying* (in time and knowledge, if not in actual dollars or pounds) *to not receive* advertising. The 2016 YouGov poll[65] says that 22 per cent of British adults are using ad-blocking software, up from 18 per cent six months ago and 15 per cent a year ago. In fact, in January 2016 the mobile network Three claimed it would be the first UK mobile operator to block adverts. Now Apple and Samsung are following suit by letting users make the choice to prevent ads from running on their hardware. It has been called 'Adpocalypse Now' and it spells doom for advertisers.

And marketers agree. According to HubSpot – an inbound marketing software leader – *even marketers* rank paid advertising as the #1 most overrated marketing tactic.

Here's the problem:

Our world is noisy, and there's enormous competition for people's attention. Never mind the daily advertising to which we are exposed, there's the whole of the internet to contend with. In fact, there's more data available online that any single person could ever consume. To put this in perspective, here is a quote from Erik Qualman. Known as the father of 'Socialnomics' (social economics), he has been producing annual statistics about social media and the state of our world. As far back as 2012, he said that 'If Wikipedia were made into a book it would be 2.25 million pages long, and would take over 123 years to read.' That's *just* Wikipedia: only one of the billions of sources of information available on the internet to read, consume and distract our employees every moment. Remember, this statistic comes from 2012. The amount of data availability has grown enormously since then.

HOW DOES ANYONE ACTUALLY GET HEARD?

With all this competition, how can companies make sure that their messages actually get to the right places? Well, companies have a unique advantage here – they have the dedicated attention of their employees eight hours a day or so, five days a week.

And this is why, when it comes to employee engagement, companies have to think very differently these days. Instead of 'shouting' at their employees and expecting mindless, automaton-like responses, they've had to become listeners.

Great examples abound of companies who have turned themselves around by listening to their employees. Toyota, anecdotally, encourages every single employee (from a cleaner to a CEO) to stop a production line if they spot an error or mistake, or simply see a better way of doing it. It's part of their kaizen approach. Ricardo Semler at Semco encouraged his employees to choose working hours that suited them – even the people working in manufacturing plants did this.[66] And it worked. Profits increased dramatically, people were happier about their working conditions, and productivity increased too.

But listening to your employees only works if the messages your employees are brave enough to give you *actually get filtered through to the decision-makers in a way that matters*. It's all very well having a 'CEO open forum' or an 'open door policy', but if employees don't believe that they will actually be heard, or that what they have to say will be taken seriously, not many people are likely to come forward.

It's not easy, for sure, because some employees prefer to stay below the radar, others don't believe they'll be heard or believed, still others think that they'll be persecuted for their honest opinions and some, well, they just like to complain perpetually. The risk of a truly open door policy is that it may very well attract some whingers. In truth, it probably will.

WHINGERS VS. TRUTH-TELLERS

The whinger is the one who has had a horrible journey in this morning, as he does almost every day. He's the one who complains that he's sick, or about to get sick – and this happens regularly. He's the individual who whines about his life, his partner who doesn't appreciate him, and his dog, who he loves but is always creating a mess. In his life, everything is too much trouble.

The chances are that just about everyone knows someone like this in their office. Even in great companies, where extra care and attention is taken to recruit high-calibre individuals, there will always be some people whose lives just seem to go wrong all the time. They seem to get their pleasure in life by sharing their misery with others under the mistaken assumption that people care about their problems – or, perhaps, that people will continue caring no matter how much they complain. So, initially, some of their colleagues will give them sympathy, but in the long term, more and more colleagues will ignore them, until only the really long-suffering colleagues are prepared to smile, listen politely, and try to escape from their (inevitably long-winded and dull) conversation before it sucks them in and sucks the life out of them.

But then there are the truth-tellers. It is because of these rare, high-calibre individuals that open door policies *should* exist.

The truth-teller is the kind of person who will always keep calm in meetings. He's the one who is always polite and respectful. He'll never argue (at least, not in the open), but you can tell that something's going on behind the façade of politeness. You can tell, from the occasional insightful comments in meetings that surprise you for their rarity as much as their ability to nail the exact essence of the argument, that there's a very big brain under there – and huge potential to identify opportunities to change for the better.

Unlike the whinger, ignore the truth-teller at your peril! This is the kind of employee who managers actively need to take the time to seek out, listen to and encourage to go beyond their job role – because they're the ones who see what's really going on.

Perhaps, in time, they'll start their own company or find opportunities to lead in businesses that give them a sense of direction. But for now, if they don't have a way to share the insights they're silently generating, then your company is making a big mistake that could have enormous repercussions in lost opportunities.

THE VALUE OF LISTENING

The truth-tellers are often ignored because they're quiet. They'll listen first and speak second – if at all. But it's arguably more important to elicit information from them than from anyone else in the team, because they know that listening is an art.

Listening isn't just about shutting up long enough to hear what someone else is saying, although that's a start. In reality, most people in a conversation will only spend half their time listening (while they're thinking about what they're going to say next) and, as a result, they often miss the 'truth' these truth-absorbers pick up. Quite simply, truth-absorbers are able to absorb information because they spend more time listening than they spend planning what they're going to say next. They know that great listening is also about hearing *what's not being said*. It's about processing body language, identifying hidden clues that belie people's true intentions, and sussing out the power struggles that underlie the words.

There's a difference between people who don't speak simply because they don't have anything to say and those who have a lot to say but don't feel like it's appropriate for them to say it. These truth-absorbers are often deeply insightful – if the loudmouths will shut up long enough for them to get a word in edgeways.

All that listening and silent thinking allows them to process and draw inferences from seemingly unrelated data. In this way, they become remarkably good strategists – far more so than anyone realises.

The surprising thing about good strategists, actually, is that they can exist at any or all levels of your business, regardless of their age, experience, training or background. They simply see the world in a different way. For them, the world is simpler. Solutions that are obvious to them wouldn't even occur to those who seek immediate solutions, lack patience or spend their time talking rather than listening.

GOOD STRATEGY IS OBVIOUS TO THE TRUTH-OBSERVERS

I'm not one of them, but I've spent a lot of time with them. They're not just highly intelligent; they also have a genuinely different way of processing information. As a result, they often become frustrated by others who *can't* see what they see. They don't understand that what they have is both a blessing and a curse. They're blessed by the ability to see the wood itself rather than just the trees, and cursed by the fact that they either can't communicate how to get through the forest, can't convince people to go down a certain woodland path, or aren't trusted enough – or given the opportunities – to show others how simple the path really would be to navigate if it was taken.

They also threaten managers because they challenge the status quo.

These are the very people businesses need to pay attention to. Fortunately, now that we live in a new era of authenticity, it has become popular, trendy even, to pay attention to your employees – which we'll discuss further in the next section. The challenge lies in determining how to find the *right* employees to listen to, not least because the truth-tellers are more inclined to listen than to speak. Leaders and managers in business have to find a way for employees to feel comfortable enough to speak the truth. It's not easy, but it starts by giving all employees a voice, and then finding the nuggets of truth in amidst the alluvial stream of random ideas, whinges and well-intentioned but irrelevant input.

IT'S TIME TO LISTEN TO YOUR EMPLOYEES MORE

It's not just good practice to listen to your employees to find out what your company can do better. A good employee-listening programme that is taken seriously is actually a sign of a company where employees *want* to work. As companies seek to differentiate themselves in an increasingly competitive job market, it's becoming ever more important to find strategic differentiators. Listening to and, more importantly, acting on those suggestions is one way of being strategically different.

This listening is also important because what management assumes is the case down 'in the ranks' – or what they observe and misconstrue from their lofty levels of seniority – is seldom the truth, and certainly not the whole truth and nothing but the truth. This honest and open feedback is imperative because companies can no longer afford to misrepresent themselves to their prospective employees, whether intentionally or unintentionally. As well as having low to no tolerance of dishonesty, employees, quite frankly, have too much choice. If they don't like what they see when they start a job and it doesn't represent the advertised reality, they won't stay.

No-one assumes they will have a 'job for life' any more. Financial crises, having multiple bread-winners in one family, the opportunity for companies to make use of redundancies when their bottom line isn't looking healthy enough for shareholders, and a lack of loyalty from employers, all mean that employees *can no longer expect* to have a job for life any more.

However, it goes both ways. Employers no longer expect their employees to stay with them forever, either. The increase in the number of recruitment agencies and job boards, the fluidity of the market and the attention span of many employees makes changing jobs far easier now than it was decades ago. So, companies have to make themselves desirable. This means, first that they must find a way to represent their best side to both their employees and their customers.

WAYS TO HELP YOUR TRUTH-TELLERS 'SPEAK OUT'

Here are a few pointers to encourage your truth-tellers to be open and frank. It starts at the top.

- Tell the truth: to each other, to your managers, to your customers.

- Hold every single leader to an even higher level of accountability for honesty and inventiveness than everyone else in the business.
- Don't squash ideas!
- Give your employees the opportunity to point out things that don't work or could be done better.
- Be aware that your company's brand is being represented beyond the boundaries of the office walls. Employees reflect their employers in their lives away from the office.
- Hire the right people that fit with your company.
- Realise that a great workplace culture can be cultivated, that it will attract a certain type of person, but not everyone will want to fit into that mould. Work to keep people, but also let them go when it's time.
- Actively seek out truth-tellers. Don't flinch from their honest commentary; encourage it.

This requires an enormous amount of openness and humility – as well as the ability to be wrong and the courage to accept the fact that managers and senior leaders (especially the CEO) are not always the best at everything. There's always room for improvement and, more often than not, when encouraged and given the right combination of resources and guidance, employees can create amazing and innovative solutions to potential problems.

> **LESSON 7:** Your truth-tellers are a source of surprising insight and potential strategy that can power or inspire your Secret Army. Listen to them.

Key Takeaways:

- *Marketing isn't about lying, it's about giving messages to your customers and prospects in a way that helps them help themselves.*

- *Marketing should be every CEO's ally but don't forget that it can be used both ways: to spread messages and to listen, both internally and externally.*

- *Seek out and pay attention to your company's truth-tellers. It's not easy, but it has to start with giving all employees a voice, and then finding the nuggets of truth amidst the alluvial stream of random ideas, whinges and well-intentioned but irrelevant input.*

Chapter 9: Guerrilla Leaders

What happens when the leadership of your Secret Army fails? This chapter reveals the concept of absentee landlords (why your employees are your tenants), guerrilla leaders and the butterfly-in-a-box syndrome.

Have you ever watched the film *The Devil's Advocate*? It's a chilling tale about humans and the devil. In it, there's a scene where Satan goes on a tirade against God, calling him an absentee landlord.

This phrase, the concept of an absentee landlord, stuck with me long after most of the film had been forgotten.

ABSENTEE LANDLORDS

When landlords aren't there to maintain, oversee and generally look after their properties, the places fall into disrepair. Occasionally, landlords are fortunate enough to have careful or caring tenants who look after the property as if it were their own, but these are the exception rather than the rule.

Some landlords solve the problem by employing a management company. This company's objective is to maintain the property to a suitable standard while keeping costs down for both themselves and the owners. In this case, when an absentee landlord is replaced by a substitute landlord, it simply means that while the properties won't fall down, they usually won't have that 'loved' feeling either.

I know a pair of excellent landlords. They choose their tenants carefully, vet them, interview them, ask for a longer-term commitment than average and, when their tenants leave, it's almost like a member of their family has departed. They choose tenants who love their properties, who truly feel like the places they live in are home, even if they are just living in rented accommodation, and even if they're only there for a year or so. These tenants buy in to the places in which they live, even if they don't actually buy them. Some tenants have even offered to paint the walls, or pay for them to be painted out of their own pockets, or do other minor property improvements because they feel like they have a stake in the place in which they live – not just because they don't like having white walls. At the end of the day, though, they're still tenants, so they won't pay for a boiler to be repaired if it breaks, or for an upgrade to facilities.

The difference between having tenants who love a place and those who merely live in a place is marked. Tenants who treat a rented property as if it is their home spend more time, care and attention on it. They take more pride in it. And the places are invariably cleaner, better maintained and in better nick when the tenants eventually move on – as all tenants do.

So, what makes these landlords great? And what does property rental have to do with a book about the Secret Army that can make or break the success of your company?

YOUR EMPLOYEES ARE YOUR TENANTS

Your employees 'rent' your property for the duration of their employment. They can be good or bad tenants. Likewise, in your company, the leaders are your landlords. It's up to them to decide whether they want to be active landlords, or simply leave the rental to a management company. It's possible to encourage your employees to stay on by making their environment welcoming, by encouraging a sense of ownership in their work or, even, by offering share options that literally make them part-owners in the business.

The other side of this analogy deals with the bad tenants. If you've ever heard nightmare stories about what people can get up to in rented accommodation, trust me, they're true. The damage that people can do to properties they don't care about is incredible and, unfortunately, even the most carefully-selected tenants can get nasty and vindictive when they believe they aren't treated fairly. Stories range from simple carelessness (cigarette burns on the carpet, gouges and scrapes on the walls), to locking landlords out of the property and doing malicious damage.

The thing is, people are people. Some people are naturally inclined to treat things with respect, to take pride in their place of residence (or their work), and others aren't. Both landlords and company owners/leaders have a responsibility to choose the right tenants, build a sense of pride in the place where they live/work, and then empower them to feel – for the duration of their stay – that they have a 'stake' or a sense of 'ownership' in that place.

When they do – when employees are empowered, know where they're going, and understand why they're going in that direction and how they fit into the bigger picture – then things run significantly more smoothly.

But what happens when employees don't know where they're going, or feel like they aren't being led? Does chaos ensue? Actually, no. Generally, businesses keep on going. Employees keep on working on tasks (after all, they're paid to do a job). But companies lose focus and then, occasionally, something weird happens. Guerrilla leaders pop up.

guerrilla / noun
- A member of a small independent group taking part in irregular fighting, typically against larger regular forces.
- Referring to actions or activities performed in an impromptu way, often without authorisation.

– OxfordDictionaries.com

GUERRILLA LEADERSHIP

These days the term guerrilla is used in at least four contexts: guerrilla warfare, guerrilla marketing[q], guerrilla gardening –

---

[q] This is not to be confused with 'gorilla marketing' which is also a term, believe it or not. Gorilla marketing describes one of the first examples of viral advertising on the internet. It refers to the Cadbury's chocolate advert in which a gorilla played the drums. What this had to do with chocolate I'm not entirely sure but it certainly made the Cadbury's regal purple regalia a global phenomenon, as people all over the world shared this video with their friends, and their friends shared it with colleagues, and colleagues shared it with relatives etc. etc. until millions had watched this advert of a large gorilla beating his heart out. I don't know why.

and now, guerrilla leadership. The root of the word (*guerre*) comes from the French word for war, but it's not just about out-and-out war; it's about sneaky tactics to subvert an enemy when the numbers are against you.

The French guerrillas in the Second World War called themselves freedom fighters, and both terms are used in wars and skirmishes all over the world today. Usually, the concept 'freedom fighter' has a positive connotation, while guerrilla has connotations that are more pejorative. Regardless, the tactic occurs when the guerrillas don't have the power, but they have the desire to make change and the ingenuity to act on it in surprising ways.

A few years ago, the term guerrilla marketing (also known as ambush marketing) made its way into common parlance. One of the earliest instances of guerrilla marketing was when a brand 'hijacked' their opposition's sponsored event (the American Super Bowl) by handing out thousands of free t-shirts emblazoned with their own logo. Since people don't turn down a free t-shirt, the result was an entire stadium filled with the competitor's t-shirts on one of the most important sponsorship days of the year. Imagine the anger of the legitimate sponsor, who had paid millions of dollars for exclusive sponsorship rights, when 'their' event was effectively stolen by their biggest rival?

Another interesting example of the term 'guerrilla' being used in common parlance is guerrilla gardening – or, what Ron Finley calls 'gangsta gardening'.

He wanted to flip the term 'gangsta' on its head just like the term 'guerrilla' can sometimes be flipped on its head and used in a positive way to embrace change for the better.

This is Ron's story.

Usually people associate 'gangsta' with bad things – with violence and murder. But according to a wonderful discussion I had with Ron, he wanted to change the associations. He says,[67] 'Being educated is Gangsta. Having knowledge is Gangsta. Being self-sustaining – that's Gangsta. Providing for your community is Gangsta. The soil is Gangsta, Mother

Nature is Gangsta' and that's what we want to embrace!'[r]

When Ron gave a TED talk[68] about gardening in South Los Angeles – where there is huge food disparity, by design – he wanted to point out that poor food consumption is not happenstance. Somebody designed the fact that the stores that serve garbage food are everywhere; and they're making billions and billions of dollars out of the fact that good food is really hard to find.

He says that ghettoes are made to be poor – it's a function of the design. Likewise, Ron says, 'we have a food problem by design'.

But if neighbourhoods can be designed around poor food consumption, it also means that things can be changed to promote good food and good health, by design.

Ron has proven that this design can be changed through the innovative and subversive tactic of *growing your own food* (Gasp! Shock! Horror!). Actually, he started growing food, very subtly, very quietly, on sidewalks. There was land. There were hungry people. There were other people who were prepared to put the effort in to grow the food – and so they did.

He says, 'It's very simple. Beauty in, beauty out. It's not just about healthy food – it's about a healthy environment. If you've got healthy food but a horrible place that you live in, that's going to affect your health. Not everyone is putting those two pieces together. People say, 'eat your fruit and vegetables,' but that could be killing you too. If you don't know where it comes from, you don't know what it's sprayed with.'

To go back to the story, when people started growing food 'Gangsta-style' in Ron's neighbourhood, amazing things happened. At first, people were reluctant to eat food out of these free gardens. Then they started taking part and helped to grow more food. Then they started taking pride in their environment, and then it became a movement – influencing the way people thought and felt about food, vegetables, *and*

---

[r] I am deeply indebted to Ron himself, and Ashleigh Carter of The Ron Finley Project, for spending the time with me to make sure this extract reflects Ron's true philosophy.

the environment in which they lived. 'Kids who grow tomatoes eat tomatoes,' Ron says. It's a movement towards health, fuelled by the power of strawberries! ('Plus, they taste good,' he adds.)

Ron grew food in opposition to food poverty and food injustice, and he has created a global food movement. But any guerrilla movement only becomes successful once enough people act, intelligently, to make a difference. With guerrilla marketing, it only works if people wear the t-shirts. With guerrilla warfare, it only works if enough freedom fighters take subversive action. And with guerrilla leadership, well, here's how it works at companies where leadership is lacking.

If the situation is dire enough, if there is no clear sense of business strategy or direction, no clear objectives, and if people get a sense that things are simply hopeless, one of two things happen.

- People give up. They go to work, spend most of their time on Facebook, Snapchat (or whatever the latest popular social media channel is), do the barest minimum, and go home, bored, frustrated and annoyed.
- They fight.

Sometimes, situations arise where employees feel strongly enough about a core element of the business that they choose to protect it. When this happens, guerrilla teams can form. Their identity becomes anti-establishment; ironically, because they *do* identify with the establishment's original values but don't believe that management is currently demonstrating those values. If they don't see any reason to do what management is telling them to do, or worse, if they truly believe that what management is telling them to do is *wrong*, then they will start to fight against it.

The guerrilla teams see themselves in a war against the power structure that they believe is causing the undesirable status, and they start taking guerrilla-like actions (as defined at the beginning of this chapter). Firstly, they'll identify themselves as separate from the management team and as 'member[s] of a small independent group'. This gives them a new identity and a sense of collaborative purpose. Being in opposition to the 'large, regular force' (senior management) gives them the belief that they have to fight for what they think is right. Secondly, if they haven't already been doing this, they'll start taking action in impromptu ways that aren't endorsed by the current management team. The interesting or dangerous part, depending on your perspective, happens when they start doing things without authorisation but in an organised, dedicated way. Read on for an example...

GUERRILLA LEADERSHIP REQUIRES A RINGLEADER

Going from a small group of dissatisfied whingers to a fully-formed guerrilla coup requires a 'ring leader' – someone who is in a position of reasonable authority and has decided to take a stand.

It requires a lot to create a guerrilla leader: it means that they've been pushed long enough or hard enough, or there has been a significant enough event to have pushed them over the edge, to a point where they take matters into their own hands.

I've known guerrilla leadership to occur when there is a perfect storm with several of the following conditions:

- lack of leadership from high up in the business,
- the presence of determined and charismatic sub-leaders,
- the support of subordinates, or an 'army' of followers, who have more faith in the sub-leader than in the higher leader (it doesn't need to be a large army, a few 'believers' will suffice),
- a boiling pot of dissent and frustration, or
- a ticking time-bomb of impatience that has not been addressed, and which the guerrilla team feels will not be addressed by any other means.

Guerrilla leadership happens more often than you might think, but it usually doesn't amount to anything because the guerrilla sub-groups themselves don't amount to much. There may be dissent, a lack of leadership, impatience and frustration in a business, but one or more of the key ingredients required to build a strong opposition movement is lacking. Usually, the guerrilla leader is not strong enough; they don't have a clear enough sense of what they want to achieve – they're more focused on moving *away* from what they don't want than *towards* something they do want – they aren't prepared to act and stick to it; or they don't have a plan.

I knew a guerrilla leader, once. They did it intentionally. They had a plan, a following, an opportunity, the determination to do it and, even, tacit approval from the senior leader. The irony is that the senior leader didn't realise this was a bid to overcome his lack of leadership (or, at least, the guerrilla leader didn't think he did). But, like all failed military coups, this one ended badly. The senior leader eventually realised that his company's direction was being led by marketing, not by himself, and he clamped down on the 'dissidents' who, by that stage, had inspired and fired-up most of the business far beyond the realms of traditional marketing influence or activity. And the guerrilla activities stopped. In retrospect, what probably tipped him off was the fact that many of his employees were more interested in getting involved in marketing initiatives than they were in working towards the either unachievable, un-scoped or badly-led projects that earned the company's bread and butter.

The guerrilla leader explained to me that they didn't regret being a guerrilla leader, or the fact that things changed significantly once they were 'found out', because guerrilla leadership is sometimes necessary in order for the company to have a wake-up call.

The guerrilla leader in this case was responsible for marketing, but frustrated leaders can appear in any guise, and in any company.

BUTTERFLY IN A BOX

I first came across the concept of 'butterfly in a box' at an academic institution with large grounds and beautiful gardens. The grounds and gardens manager had a tough job managing and inspiring large teams of very poorly paid gardeners and maintenance workers to maintain the quality associated with a leading academic institution. This leader, however, knew a lot about managing people. And so, when he came across one individual who was a wannabe guerrilla leader, rather than stomping down hard on him (as tyrants typically do), he promoted him.

I'll never forget what he said to me: 'Sometimes angry, frustrated trouble-makers aren't trying to do damage. They're just leaders looking for a place to lead.'

He used the analogy of a butterfly in a box. If you try to trap a butterfly in your hands, or in a box, they frantically flutter around, trying to escape. But, once you let them free – either into a larger container or completely remove the restrictions – they calm down and stay where they are.

This gardener looking for a place to lead was a butterfly. He needed to vent, to express his dissatisfaction. He had complaints. But he also had ideas, and charisma. He was a trouble-maker precisely because his leadership abilities were being thwarted.

Once he was let out of a box into a field where he could fly free and lead people, he calmed down. His behaviour transformed from that of a trouble-maker to that of an invaluable team member – purely because he was now able to make decisions, implement ideas, and represent the people in his team as a leader should.

The sceptic in me acknowledges that he may not have been comfortable with his new location or role for long, but the optimist in me likes to think of the story having a happy ending. I like to think of this man creating beautiful new gardens, inspiring the others in his team to see the meaning in their work, and that (for a time, anyway) everyone in the team went home with a sense of satisfaction and achievement – because he was leading them towards something they were inspired to achieve.

> **LESSON 8:** Sometimes the trouble-makers in your army are just leaders looking for a place to lead. Don't simply discipline them or, worse, kick them out. Give them more responsibility.

Key Takeaways:

- *Your employees are your tenants. Are you managing them well, so they feel a sense of ownership and pride in your property?*

- *Guerrilla leadership can develop when there's a lack of leadership, the presence of determined or charismatic sub-leaders, the support of an army of followers and a ticking time-bomb of impatience that has not been addressed by any other means.*

- *Guerrilla leaders can start a tide of productive change if, rather than keeping these 'butterflies in a box', they are given the freedom to lead in their own context.*

Chapter 10: Frustrated Storytellers

Why do we need office popcorn makers? It's linked to why humans are programmed to be social, the evolutionary importance of connecting on a human level, and why storytelling is so important in leadership. In this chapter, we talk about who storytellers are, who they should be, and how to capture and release frustrated storytellers' insights in a way that changes business for the better.

SOCIAL CONNECTIONS

The human brain is designed to make connections. Author Matthew D. Lieberman, who wrote *Social: Why Our Brains Are Wired to Connect*,[69] has found evidence that when our brains are 'resting', our default state is set so that our brains are actively processing and making meaning of our relationships, putting them into context and organising our world. His analysis of FMRI (functional magnetic resonance imaging) scans indicates that the human evolutionary advantage does not come just from our prehensility (our agile fingers and toes), but from mammalian group advantage too. In other words, social connection.

This social connection is about forming bonds between team members. A range of mammalian groups have it: monkeys, dolphins, humans and others.

The evidence from Lieberman's research suggests that, apart from the advantages of larger brains and opposable thumbs, our ability to connect with others and form groups is partly (or mostly) what has allowed us to evolve.

Imagine you are a member of a tribe of one of our near evolutionary ancestors: monkeys. They do have tribes, and their tribes have leaders. Leaders defend the group from predators, keep them safe, find good hunting/feeding grounds and fight off other troops. They have to do it or the troop dies. So, collaborating provides an evolutionary advantage.

But monkeys, like many mammals, also have connection traits that don't seem to be merely about survival. At close of day, when the sun goes down, they can be seen huddling together, cuddling and grooming. Almost as if they were reflecting on the day. They are social. So are we.

> Does feeling socially connected make people socialise more and work less, or does it make team members work harder because they feel more responsibility for the team's success?... Neuroscience research indicates that ignoring social well-being is likely to harm team performance (and individual health) for reasons we would not have guessed.
>
> – Matthew D. Lieberman

GREAT BUSINESSES RECOGNISE THE NEED TO CONNECT ON A HUMAN LEVEL

There's a trend in successful businesses these days, particularly among tech startups, to provide in-office business perks that are increasingly more unusual and, yet, increasingly designed to foster community, collaboration and social integration.

Google's London offices are legendary for their funky décor, 'nap pods' and their free lunches. Similarly, some companies now feature full-on gyms for their employees. Other offices feature slides, multi-function cola fountains, popcorn machines and other cool tools that make their employees feel a bit more loved.

Having a workplace that creates a certain vibe – of creativity and fun – certainly fosters a specific type of working mentality. I've seen it in evidence. One startup I worked for encouraged clubs for everything you could imagine (just about). In one week I discovered they had a book club, a cheese club, and even a pancake club. Individuals started a club, the company would contribute something towards the club (providing it was a good idea, fitted within the company ethos and had enough interest from staff members), and then people joined in and collaborated.

Clubs, food and fancy office features are great – but they're a symptom rather than the cause of an open, collaborative environment. Someone makes the decision to put these cool tools and collaborative toys in place (yes, really, toys! Many companies have football tables, even ping-pong tables, or Wii competitions). Someone, usually the head of HR with the support of senior management, or senior management themselves, decides that it makes good financial sense to 'waste' money on gimmicks and office freebies – and it does!

Happier employees are more motivated. Employees who can take breaks when they need to are more productive. Even flexible working is a symptom, ironically, of fostering group collaboration. It allows people to be human and, as a result, when they're working they're fully working, not distracted by issues at home. It means that when they do work flexible hours, more often than not the company gets more working time out of its employees than they take off. In fact, many people who have swapped a long commute for a work-from-home lifestyle have simply ended up translating most of their commute time into working time. Yet it works for them, because they don't have to fight with traffic or public transport and crowds, and they're less stressed as a result.

However, there are things they lose by never being in the office, one of which is the ability to interact with other people. This time spent in the office kitchen builds social links and improves group cohesion. This, in turn, improves connectivity, understanding and collaboration.

One of the things that we do, most often, when standing around waiting for a kettle to boil or for the coffee to brew is swap stories – about our weekends, our lives, our frustrations and the world around us. It's part of human evolution. Storytelling is one of the ways in which social well-being is fostered: by creating, maintaining and enhancing a sense of group collaboration.

It is human nature to try to make sense of our world. People tell stories in order to do that. What Lieberman's FMRI scans discovered is that humans are *almost always* telling themselves stories in order to make meaning of events, from the simplest to the most complex.

If people are lucky, their parents raised them on bedtime stories. Certainly, our distant ancestors made meaning around the fireside by telling themselves and their tribe-members stories too. Storytelling is in our DNA.

Just because people are supposed to behave differently at work than they do in their private lives doesn't mean that we should ignore the role of stories or relegate them to the 'not helpful here' pile. Businesses can benefit from storytelling as much, or even more, than individuals do, because stories can take very complex subjects and both simplify and contextualise them. Great leaders are able to do the same.

Some of the most memorable addresses I've ever heard from business leaders were when they used stories, not just numbers, to get their point across.

I'll never forget the first time I ever saw someone use a PowerPoint presentation that was entirely devoid of bullet points, or even text. It wasn't a highly conceptual or purely motivational presentation. It was a quarterly review. But it had no numbers or words to encapsulate the company's successes and direction – it just had pictures. That doesn't mean that the content was lacking. Rather, every piece of information was there – just spoken out loud, with each image making perfect sense in context. These single images were underpinned by great stories that made the presenter's point far more clearly than dry, word-stuffed slides ever would have. This is because a picture really does tell a thousand words, and can encapsulate all sorts of memories and connotations that help drive a story home. It's why TED has become such a global phenomenon: it's based on the ability of individuals to engage others *by telling their personal stories*.

So, what stories does a business need to tell itself in order to justify treating its employees in a way that optimises productivity and creates cohesion?

In Section 2, we talked about the benefits of getting employees on board by inspiring them to have meaning in their work so that they know where the company is going and what their role is within the company's larger plans. A very important part of getting employees on board, of building those human connections and fostering productive work environments, comes down to telling stories that define acceptable behaviour and enforce 'the way we do things around here'. It's the stories you hear on the first day at the office – whether the attention to health and safety rules is conveyed in a meaningful way (if there's a fire, don't stand there and die, here's the fire exit), or rigid insistence upon arbitrary rules (you can't use the toilets on the Partners' floor). It's the way in which you're introduced to people in the business. For example, is the Head of Finance spoken about in hushed tones of awed respect, or as a human being? Victoria may be the CFO, but sometimes she's introduced as 'head of the team that makes sure our clients pay us so that we can all get paid'. I know which of those two I'd rather work with.

TELLING STORIES

Your company's story (the reason you're in business and, presumably, successful at it) underlies everything your employees do while working for you, whether they realise it or not. Companies define who they are by what they stand for, and also by what they choose to not do, to not tell, or to actively dissuade people from doing.

Some startups that make it big will use the inspiration of their founders as a driving force behind their success. Concur, for example, was extremely proud of the fact that their three co-founders started the business in someone's living room. Their spirit of entrepreneurship was one of the first things new employees heard about – even before they joined.

Others may choose to define their stories as they evolve. For example, HubSpot has a culture code that encapsulates their ethos and way of working. They call it 'part manifesto and part employee handbook'. At the time of writing, it was 128 slides long.[70] It includes everything from why they exist (to 'Solve for the Customer – SFTC') to their opinion on office politics ('We hate it with the heat of a thousand suns'). When people apply for jobs, they are encouraged to create another slide for the culture code, and are assessed on whether their addition makes them an ideal team member or not.

This is the blueprint for the stories their employees tell themselves while they make decisions and take action every single day. It creates a framework for what makes people proud to be part of their team.

Regardless of how it is articulated, be it in the format of the founder's story, the innovation that created their first product or the ethos that keeps them going, the story of a company's culture is often an important element in attracting the right employees in the first place.

Is it a story they buy in to? If not, then perhaps it's not the right place for them.

So, what happens when businesses have been around for a while – so long, in fact, that employees have forgotten the company's origins or no longer have a sense of what really matters to them?

There are two potential outcomes.

- The business loses focus.
- The business chooses another story.

A friend of mine joined a certain startup. He was excited about their technology, bought into their ethos and believed he could make a difference. Then he realised the company had actually been acquired by a huge conglomerate and that the company he had joined was being swallowed, bit by bit. His interesting, challenging job was transformed into a frustrating, faceless contribution towards a plan that no-one appeared to understand fully, never mind believe in. The company demonstrated almost irrational decision-making, and employees from the newly-acquired company left, in droves.

Perhaps that was their business strategy. Acquire the technology, mismanage the people, and wait for the headcount to drop. It's uncertain.

What is telling, however, is that no-one really seemed to understand their story, or their 'why' for doing things. Projects got started, then canned. Products got built, then abandoned. Groups got formed, then re-formed, then re-formed again.

The company wasn't necessarily populated only by bad leaders. They just didn't seem to have a consistent battle plan that their soldiers (employees) could follow.

Arguably, perhaps the foot-soldiers shouldn't know what the general's plan is; but someone should. Otherwise what ends up happening is that employees are treated like mushrooms: kept in the dark and fed on bullshit.

Yes, stories begin at the top of the business (arguably, we could even say that great business strategy is a series of defining 'stories'), but it isn't just the bosses who tell stories. Every single person in the organisation, and beyond – anyone who has any contact with the business – is telling his or her own stories about the business in ways we can barely begin to imagine.

For example, the lack of stories from senior management that leads to a mushroom culture does not result in a lack of stories being shared around the business. No, stories are still circulating. They just aren't the kind of stories that enable positive or productive working. They confuse more than enlighten, and they can be downright dangerous. If the businesses who use this tactic were movie-makers, then their plot would be weak, their characters purposeless and their film likely to totally flop in the theatres.

WHOSE STORIES?

So, businesses need a story, a strong story that encapsulates their ethos, to start with. But just one? No. They need multiple stories. Dozens. Hundreds. They need stories from each of the foot-soldiers in the Secret Army in order to build a successful business. In fact, they have these stories already; they just need to tap into them.

THREE GROUPS OF STORYTELLERS

Business storytellers come in three groups. Leaders are storytellers. So are customers. So are employees. Every single one of the stories they tell has the potential to inspire others to work better, identify issues that can be improved, or build a team that takes people – and the company – to new heights.

Ideally, they should be telling the same story, but from different perspectives. If anyone attached to the business hears that these stories are inconsistent or (even worse) contradictory, then they know they have a problem. However, often these stories go unheard by anyone with the power to make the changes that could turn a bad story into a good one.

The sad thing is that if no-one's listening, even the best story in the world will count for nothing. It may have the potential to change the world, inspire thousands of people, or communicate truths that could influence the future, but if no-one hears it, it might as well not have been told in the first place.

Too often there is no opportunity for the storytellers to 'speak up'. Or, if they do, they worry that they will be ignored or even fired. It is possible, however, to turn a mushroom culture into a positive one.

THE BALLAD OF PAUL O'NEILL

This story of a former CEO of Alcoa (the Aluminum Company of America), Paul O'Neill, seems naïve in many ways, but it's not. Because it's true. Charles Duhigg tells it in *The Power of Habit: why we do what we do and how to change.*[71] Duhigg tells this story so beautifully that it's worth getting a copy of the book to do it justice but, in short, it's an example of where a story – in this case, something as apparently uninspiring as worker safety – can transform a company to become one of the safest manufacturing plants in the USA *and simultaneously* see its stock price rise by more than 200 per cent.

O'Neill started with a vision: 'I intend to make Alcoa the safest company in America. I intend to go for zero injuries.' His speech to shareholders was not well received. They were expecting a speech that, as Duhigg puts it,

> …should start with an introduction, make a faux self-deprecating joke… and end[s] with a blizzard of buzzwords – "synergy," "rightsizing," and "co-opetition" – at which point everyone could return to their offices, reassured that capitalism was safe for another day.

But O'Neill's vision of safety was about to underpin fundamental changes that, amongst other things, allowed employees *at all levels of the business* to speak up about the stories in their culture that needed changing so that they *could* become the safest company in America.

Duhigg's book is not about stories, it's about habits. But habits can change because of the stories we tell ourselves about why we do what we do. At Alcoa, under the mantle of a focus on safety, employees were able to voice their concerns about unsafe practices, and be heard. Every single person in the business was empowered to share stories. Indeed, they were responsible for sharing stories about safety.

And it transformed their business.

Words, and stories, have the power to change the world.

FRUSTRATED STORYTELLERS

However, words are not everyone's friends. Many people embrace logic, maths and reasoning rather than verbal skills. To them, words may be alien, or just unmanageable. Ironically, these individuals who eschew words and embrace logic are some of the best sources of stories – precisely because they're able to get to the real nub of the story and explain the 'why' of what they do in a way that resonates with an audience like themselves.

This is where most marketers make a huge mistake: they don't capture the stories of their colleagues who think about words in an alternative way.

At one company I worked for, we did things differently, though. We actively sought out those who were time-poor but opinion-rich, who were not natural writers but were natural thinkers and problem-solvers, and we gave them a voice.

This is where a tool like Passle can prove to be so helpful. Passle is a mini-blogging platform. Their strapline is 'Passle turns busy experts into thought leaders', and they do it by removing the mental block associated with a blank page. How? Using their platform, individuals simply select the piece of an article that inspires them, and use that as the starting point for their own comment on that article. Their comment can be short or long, it can be related to the content or tangential, it can complement or disagree with the original source, but it gets people talking (and writing) and – this is the important part – allows non-wordy people to start writing and telling their own stories.

I ran a project using Passle as a way of getting insightful messages out to the rest of the business community, customer base and target audience. It was brilliant. Almost.

We started by sharing the plan for Passle with the rest of the company. Our objective was to share the word about what we did as a business – not just via the salespeople or marketing teams – but via, through, and with the developers, project managers, finance team members and user experience designers. We invited people to participate, explained the objectives, showed people how easy it was to start writing and sharing their own posts, grouped them into teams, and created a competition.

It was huge. While the marketing team had previously been able to produce around one blog post a week – and the objective was to double that number – for the duration of the competition we managed to produce an average of seven times the number of posts! The only limitation, it appeared, was how much time the marketing team had available to proof-read, approve and publish the posts.

While the project wasn't able to demonstrate the kind of results it should have in terms of revenue-generation, something surprising and important happened during the competition. New leaders emerged. People who hadn't previously thought to write were writing, and encouraging others to write. But, even stranger than that (and the reason, ultimately, that the project was an almost-brilliant success) was the fact that people participating in the competition to get their opinions 'out there' started becoming more interested in, and more focused on, communicating their opinions and triumphs at work. It became a platform for self-expression. It also helped non-marketing people get interested in how to create and share messages.

While some Passle users have had huge success – one client (a group of British financial advisors) went further than we did during our Passle project – Passle argues that their success arose, in part, because they used their email newsletters to regularly share the Passle posts they had written. This amplification of their content caused a wave of sharing, commenting and interest. Their newsletter open rates, website hits and brand awareness skyrocketed.[5] More importantly, their business grew. In fact, they were so successful that they were even invited to the British Prime Minister's residence, 10 Downing Street, to share their insights.

Without a way of sharing these frustrated storytellers' stories (in this instance, via the Passle platform), no-one would ever have known how insightful the employees in this company actually were. Given that their core product was their expertise, they created the perfect 'shop window' for themselves. And it worked.

In my project, the initiative was unfortunately not run for long enough to demonstrate a positive influence on the company's revenue, as the company's traditional sales cycle was 10 to 15 times the duration of the project. What it did, though, was give every single person who was involved a sense of purpose, teamwork and pride, and gave the company a wonderful opportunity to share the stories of its usually non-vocal employees, in their own words, in a non-threatening way.

It gave the frustrated storytellers, those people who *do* have stories to tell but are afraid to, or don't know how to tell them, a chance to have their voices heard.

There are some bright spots here that are worth mentioning, however, because while it wasn't easy for everyone, the overwhelming feeling was that it was worthwhile.

One severely dyslexic individual created the first piece of writing that he was proud of (and it was really good)! One

---

[5] It was possible to directly attribute this success to the newsletter, as the rates dropped significantly the one week of the year when the newsletter was accidentally not sent out.

FRUSTRATED STORYTELLERS   117

data analytics guy wrote, quite possibly, one of the most beautiful blog posts I've ever read. And the quality manager created several truly great posts that combined a great story with useful diagrams, helpful tools and insightful information from other sources.

So, what lessons should leaders take from this exercise? Well, if you're looking for quick ROI, this is not the answer. But, if you want to encourage people to step outside of their comfort zones and produce content that empowers them, helps build your brand and shares true insights about what your company really *can* do, then this (or something like this) is a truly worthwhile exercise… with the following warnings.

- Realise that content creation can be an important team-building exercise.
- Insights can come from surprising sources across the business. There are many excellent company spokespeople in your business who can help customers understand the product/service you sell at a deeper and more meaningful level. This will encourage them to buy, in the long term.
- Don't expect immediate results. It took eighteen months for Passle's prime case study client to get amazing responses. It will take time to build your content, amplify it and develop traction with your target audience – but it's worth it. Over time, people will look to you as a source of knowledge, you'll become a trusted advisor, and the time and effort will pay dividends.
- Define objectives and get agreement at the beginning of the exercise: make sure that stakeholders understand that the number of 'views' are important at the beginning, but that tracking how these views convert over time is also critical. Agree an ROI-deadline – but make it a long one.
- Lastly, it's worth realising that although a small amount of employees' valuable time could be spent on writing – which means they won't be doing as much of

their 'day jobs' as normal – they will get a lot out of it in the process; and so will your marketing team.

The people who took part in the Passle experiment were able to contribute amazing stories that many people in the business never even knew about, that marketers would never have thought to have asked, and that customers will have benefitted from. Additionally, the company's blog post views doubled over the time the competition was taking place, and website views increased significantly.

To me, this was a perfect example of using the stories people naturally tell themselves in their business day and pulling them together. It gave employees a voice, it allowed them to share their 'secret sauce' with an external audience, and it helped those who read the stories. In my opinion that, after all, is the point of storytelling.

> **LESSON 9:** The power of people in your Secret Army lies in the stories they tell. Stories make meaning of experiences and bring clarity and context. Empower your people; tell more stories.

Key Takeaways:

- *As humans, we need to make sense of our world. We tell stories in order to do that. What Lieberman's FMRI scans discovered is that we are almost always telling ourselves stories in order to make meaning of events, from the simplest to the most complex. Storytelling is in our DNA.*

- *Businesses can benefit from storytelling as much, or even more, than individuals do, because stories can take very complex subjects and both simplify and contextualise them, and great leaders are able to do the same – simplify and amplify.*

- *Your company's story underlies everything that people do while working, whether they realise it or not. Companies define who they are by what they stand for, and also by what they choose to not do, to not tell, or to actively dissuade people from doing.*

Chapter 11: Undiscovered Idea-generators

What do bananas have to do with expenses? This chapter answers that question, and explains why your expectations of non-creative types are wrong, how vast amounts of information enable faster idea-creation (and vetting), and why undiscovered idea generators are today's equivalent of explorers and inventors. We include the importance of bringing your 'itch' to work, and talk about the ROI on fun.

There's a game I like to play with fellow creative types. We select two completely unrelated words – one random, and one associated with our business – and we have 30 seconds to link the two and come up with a catchy blog post title that encapsulates both of them.

Let me give you an example so you can try it. Set your timer – you have 30 seconds to link these two subjects.

- Business expenses.
- Bananas.

Go.

If you're a creative type, then ideas are a dime a dozen for you. So, if creativity and idea-generation comes naturally to you, then in those 30 seconds you'll have met the challenge, and possibly even have come up with several other ideas.

Here's what I came up with in 30 seconds.

- 'Can I claim bananas on expenses?' and seven other random requests that your expenses policy should be able to answer.
- Why expenses are like bananas (a post about being slippery to track down and, sometimes, the butt of a joke).
- Five a day – good habits to help you keep on top of your expenses, and keep both your bank balance and your body healthy.

They may not be the best blog post titles in the world, but for me, a creative personality type, coming up with them is quite easy.

Admittedly, some days it takes longer, and when the creativity process isn't firing up the way it should, the results are less than splendid.

The problem with being a creative type, though, is that people expect you to be creative all the time, and the problem with being labelled a traditionally 'non-creative' type is that people don't expect you to have ideas at all.

Both expectations are wrong.

Regardless of whether ideas are a dime-a-dozen or more carefully thought out, planned, re-investigated, elaborated upon and finally delivered, the question for every single business is – and should be: are people encouraged to come up with ideas that can be business-enhancing while at work? Then, are they encouraged to put those ideas to use, to challenge the status quo, to find new (better) ways of tackling existing challenges, improving systems or simply making things more efficient?

I don't believe that many companies espoused this value a few years ago. But times are changing, and businesses need to change too. The world is full of ideas and information, but it's not enough to just create ideas. The undiscovered idea-generators in your companies should be paired with people who can use their discerning opinions to filter those ideas and come up with conclusions, back them up with data, and produce new initiatives that can build powerful new tools for the company's future success. Together, the creative and analytical types can create a new team of undiscovered idea-generators, and they consume information like a tree consumes carbon dioxide.

VAST INFORMATION ENABLES FASTER IDEA-CREATION AND VETTING

As a species, we have significantly greater access to information than we did in the past. Today, many of the things we do without needing to think too hard about – such as finding simple information – are no longer stored in our brains. Instead, we rely on a new tool: Google. The vast quantity of information available at our fingertips has allowed us to 'outsource our brains' – we no longer have to rely on being able to retain or store information in our heads, or even know where to find it in a library or book.[t] Arguably, even our ability to search is becoming diminished as Google changes their searching facilities (they would probably say they're 'simplifying them').

The point here is that our world is fast – incredibly fast. So fast in fact that, zoooom, in the time it took you to read that word, huge volumes of data have already been added to the internet. As we covered in Chapter 7, it has been said that we're living in a VUCA world – a world of Volatility, Uncertainty, Complexity and Ambiguity[72] – and that information overload is just part of the challenge facing us. As a consequence, vast quantities of information can be helpful if we can filter it and use the results in valuable ways. But we certainly need the internet to help us! Here are a few statistics to prove my point from Forbes.com.[73]

- The data volumes are exploding. More data has been created in the past two years than in the entire previous history of the human race.
- Data is growing faster than ever before, and by the year 2020, about 1.7 megabytes of new information will be created every second for every human being on the planet.
- By then, our accumulated digital universe of data will grow from the 4.4 zettabytes it is today to around 44 zettabytes, or 44 *trillion* gigabytes.
- Every second, we create new data. For example, we perform 40,000 search queries every second (on Google alone), which makes it 3.5 billion searches per day and 1.2 trillion searches per year.

---

[t] It's worth checking out this amusing infographic about 'how the internet is ruining your brain'. It's a tongue-in-cheek, yet highly accurate, portrayal of how we've gone from relying on our memories to relying on our ability to find information. http://mashable.com/2012/04/10/brain-internet-infographic/

And if you think that's impressive, how about this extract from an article featured on Silicon Republic's website in 2015,[74] entitled *More data to be created in 2019 than in history of the internet*.

> New estimates from Cisco predicting that two zettabytes of data will be generated in just one year by 2019, a new record.
>
> The estimates were part of Cisco's Visual Networking Index (VNI) Forecast, which looks at how the rate of data creation and internet usage expands year-upon-year and, from this year's estimates, the amount of growth between 2014 and 2019 will be unprecedented. By 2019, global IP Traffic will reach the dizzying heights of 168 exabytes per month, which would mark a triple increase on the 59.9 exabytes that was reached last year.
>
> If this were to prove true, the amount of data generated in 2019 will be effectively larger than almost the entire history of the internet, at least from 1984 to 2013.

In reality (in my opinion, at least), this vast plethora of data has had a meaningful impact in two areas.

- An unprecedented pace of knowledge sharing that, depending on your age and adaptability, can be either overwhelming or enthralling.
- The rapid evolution of and fundamental shift between those born pre-mobile internet, and post-mobile internet.

We have to harness this power of information.

UNDISCOVERED IDEA-GENERATORS

For as long as humanity has existed, there have been individuals who sought to change the world, to find a new way of doing things, to challenge the status quo. Centuries ago they were inventors or explorers. Today we call them entrepreneurs; and thanks to the evolution and availability of information, even ordinary employees are now explorers *and* inventors *and* a hundred things besides that. It's our job, as leaders of our Secret Army, to find their hidden talents and expose them.

But not just for their sake, oh no! It's perfectly possible to pretend it's for their sake (and it's often phrased like this) but, really, it's about improving business to make more money, keep the business alive, and keep stakeholders, shareholders and board members happy. If it just happens to make employees feel motivated and inspired at the same time, that's great.

It works for Google. As we mentioned in Chapter 5, Google reputedly sets aside 20 per cent of all employees' time for alternative creative avenues. And it has paid dividends. I've heard that Google Glass was originally a '20%' project.

It works for 3M. The Post-it note was reputedly a failure, originally. Legend has it that it was supposed to be a super-strong adhesive and ended up being a super-weak adhesive, but it has saved the lives of millions of forgetful individuals as a result, metaphorically if not literally.

It works for anyone with a side project.

Ideas exist all over our businesses in the heads of unique individuals who I like to call idea-generators. Some businesses are great at harnessing the power of their employees to change the world and use their insights for significant commercial gain. Others aren't. But we owe it to ourselves and our companies to actively seek them out – particularly those who aren't often willing to speak up: the *undiscovered* idea-generators.

Our undiscovered idea-generators aren't just creative types, they're also data-filterers. They're techie and non-techie. They're either quiet or loud. They might be thinking about ideas to improve your office environment, your product set or your marketing tactics. Regardless of when or where they're producing these ideas, though, they are using a combination of two resources to do it:

- their own brains, and
- the data on the internet.

These undiscovered idea-generators are able to help our human, and our business, evolution in surprising new ways because they have access to information that can help them come up with ideas, and they're sharing information. In fact, there's so much data sharing that it can be a bit overwhelming to some. That's precisely why we need the undiscovered idea-generators in our companies, and why we need to provide them with contexts in which they can work with others around them to help vet those ideas.

BRINGING YOUR 'ITCH' TO WORK

These days, American marketing literature seems to imply that almost every employee has a 'side project' that occupies their waking hours while they're not at work. In fact, more than one person at a startup I worked at actually had their own small business that they ran entirely 'on the side'. While I'm not entirely sure how the financial technology company could benefit from the out-of-hours activity of the highly talented and intelligent employee who also runs a catering business (at least, not directly), the indirect benefits come back down to two things.

- Intelligent, motivated people need challenges, so keeping themselves challenged outside of working hours is a good thing.
- Thinking about how to make life better, or achieve goals outside of work, helps encourage employees to 'lead a big life'.[u]

People are not one-dimensional. In Chapter 5, we covered the point about doing the thing that makes you come alive (I call it your 'itch' – the thing that you would do even if no-one paid you to do it, the thing that you love, that makes life worth

---

[u] I first heard this phrase 'lead a big life' in a presentation given by Elena Donio, now the CEO of Axiom and previously the first female President of Concur. It means doing things that fire you up, both inside and outside of work.

living for you). The best workplaces are those where people get to bring their itch to work, and then use their hidden talent or passion to make a difference in their work environment.

But it goes both ways.

The worlds of work and non-work are blurring, and have been doing so ever since the smartphone started dominating our daily lives. Although there has been pushback about this merging from countries such as France, for many employees it is still almost impossible to separate work from life. Many employers expect that their employees will be available practically 24/7 to reply to emails and address work queries (even while on vacation!). So it's fair to assume that, at least some of the time, while employees are not actively focused on the work task at hand, they'll be thinking about their side projects. If their side projects are related to their work and can benefit both their work and personal lives, so much the better!

IDEA-GENERATION TIME FOR CREATIVE AND NON-CREATIVE TYPES

A startup I worked with encouraged all of its developers to have 'hack days'. This is, in my opinion, a great combination of strategy, employee motivation and time-management.

With the incessant pressures of delivering to a deadline, those 'make it better' projects (as opposed to the 'get it done yesterday' projects) always fall by the wayside. This company actively encourages their technical teams to spend one day a month on making the product better. It's creative time for non-creatives. It's a chance for them to 'play a game' with their work.

Similarly, while creative types can play with words and throw ideas around without the need for extra resources (at least, not physical ones), they too need time to share and exchange inspiration with others in order to get the creative juices flowing. The difference is that creativity in their work is much harder to justify in terms of new product development and ultimate customer value.

But great leaders know that having fun isn't just a perk of a good business with the luxury of time on its hands and discretionary spend in the budget for 'teambuilding'. 'Fun' doesn't have a tangible return on investment (ROI), but it is necessary to build and enhance productive teams.

WHAT'S THE ROI ON FUN?

A few years ago, I spoke at the BrightTALK and Spiceworks Technology Marketers Meet-Up.[75] They gave me a stuffed dinosaur toy to say thanks. Don't get me wrong, it's a cool dinosaur, but what exactly is the purpose of a bright orange T-Rex?

Its purpose, as it turns out, is inspirational.

Inspiration is necessary. In our results-obsessed world, there's a risk that even marketers, who work in the part of the business that is supposed to be a bit quirky, weird and colourful, have started to take themselves too seriously. While we do need to have metrics to account for the value of every piece of output, there's a risk that the quality of our creative work will decline if we forget how to have fun.

It is now common knowledge that motivated employees are likely to work harder and be more productive, which not only builds a more efficient and motivated workforce (which allows for greater inspiration and, quite frankly, more work done in less time), but also helps create a unique culture that makes people want to do more, be more and achieve more.

So why aren't more businesses letting their employees have fun?

There's a simple answer. It's called the Fun Police.

Apparently this is a conversation one of the marketers at the Technology Marketers Meet-Up has actually had. It went something like this:

> Marketer: 'Let's do this cool thing!'
> Fun Police: 'Why?'
> Marketer: 'Because it's fun!'
> Fun Police: 'What's the ROI on fun?'

Well, if we're honest, there is no ROI on fun, just like there's no ROI on brand awareness, employee and customer engagement, community building, brand loyalty and good feelings. But that hasn't stopped marketers from doing fun things in the past, and it shouldn't stop anyone – in marketing, sales, product development or even finance – doing it in the future. The ROI may be intangible now, but it can become exponentially valuable if it's done right.

A well-known beverage company built brand love with 'Content Marketing 2020'. Dove built brand love with 'Real Beauty Sketches'. But did either of those initiatives help them sell more of their products? Possibly. It's just highly difficult to measure the direct ROI of such brand-defining and people-helping projects, especially at the time. Why? Because brand awareness is hard to measure, but even harder to live without. You see, it turns out that, actually, there IS an ROI on fun! It's just practically impossible to measure.

As with any benefit given to employees, there has to be a balance and appropriate pay-off to 'fun time'. Employers will not carry on giving 'freebies' – whether that is time to work on company-related side projects, free food or time off (for example, for education and training purposes) – unless there's something in it for them. So far, the success of companies with highly motivated employees is showing that treating your employees well does pay dividends – literally.

So, today, I challenge you: do something fun for a change! Take your team out for a walk around the park (it's free, but you get bonus points if you buy them an ice-cream too). Or try something cool and innovative (and, dare I say it, fun!) in your marketing. Take a risk. If you're clever, you can squeeze the money out of a budget item somewhere to pay for the risky endeavour or in-work side project.

It's worth investing in fun, though, because while employees are paid for 37.5 to 40 hours of work a week, they are not paid to give their entire lives to the company. But if they're given the opportunity to 'live a big life' both inside and outside of the company, the benefits will spill over into both spheres, benefiting everyone involved.

NOT HAVING FUN IS RISKY

Conversely, there's a risk that if we don't make time to have fun, our companies will suffer. If we take ourselves too seriously; if we work so hard that we forget what life is about; if we focus so much on metrics that we forget why we're trying to produce results in the first place... there's a genuine risk that the quality of our work will suffer. But, and arguably more importantly, there's a risk that our humanity will suffer. Not least because removing the fun causes stress, which can lead to burnout, which leads to a far less motivated workforce.

Assuming that you now agree that having a motivated workforce pays dividends, the next challenge is to keep that inspiration and motivation going long after the focus has shifted to 'business as usual'. That's where the 'hidden influencers' come in, as the next chapter will show.

> **LESSON 10:** Ideas are the building-blocks of greatness. They can come from any regiment of your Secret Army – but specifically from those on the front lines. Make time for them, listen for ideas from unexpected sources and build them into business as usual.

Key Takeaways:

- *The best workplaces are those where people get to bring their 'itch' to work, and then use their hidden talent or passion to make a difference in their work environment.*

- *The Secret Army can be an amazing source of ideas if people are given permission to share them and, indeed, encouraged to participate in the business as a whole.*

- *There's a genuine risk that if we take ourselves too seriously, if we work so hard that we forget what life is about, if we focus so much on metrics that we forget why we're trying to produce results in the first place, the quality of our work will suffer and our companies will suffer as a result.*

- *Employees are paid for 37.5 to 40 hours of work a week. They're not paid to give their entire lives to the company. But if they're given the opportunity to 'live a big life' both inside and outside of the company, the benefits will spill over into both spheres, benefiting everyone involved.*

SECTION 4

A MODEL FOR INTRA-COMPANY INTEGRATION

Chapter 12: Finding the Hidden Influencers

Why do leaders fail? Who is the CEO's neck? And what does this have to do with communication? We answer these questions by talking about a few models of communication, how great leaders communicate, and who can be relied upon in an organisation to help change things for the better. We also discover the importance of cheerleaders, and talk about how important hormones and a feeling of safety are in order to help teams achieve success.

COMMUNICATION, RESPECT AND HOW STUBBORNNESS CAN KILL

A president has advisors. So do kings, queens and prime ministers. They are treated as colleagues, sometimes they're friends, and they're usually awarded the adjective of 'trusted' because they deserve it.

They exist so that those in leadership can make informed decisions based on the facts from as many relevant perspectives as possible. Advisory boards exist, in part, much like parliaments and different bodies of government exist – to prevent a senior leader from making bad decisions.

But what happens when leaders ignore their advisors?

Sometimes logical, rational solutions to problems just don't seem to be acceptable to the head of the business making the decision at the time. Not because the information isn't valid, or the arguments aren't solid, but for these four reasons:

- ego,
- lack of trust,
- already assuming they know the answers, and
- miscommunication.

In one example of a failing business I heard about, the head of the organisation was intelligent, but didn't seem to see his product or company's weaknesses. He surrounded himself with toadies and yes-men. His communication skills were lacking the moment he spoke to more than one individual at a time.

He was not a leader.

One of his employees shared their story with me and explained their view on how they had made progress at the business, not because of the leader but in spite of him.

Before my contact (who prefers to remain confidential for obvious reasons) joined the company, he was told that it was a great place to work with a vibrant culture, an impressive client list and a reputation for innovation. However, the reality was far from the idyllic picture that was portrayed, as it so often is. So he did what many motivated individuals do: he rolled up his sleeves and got to work. He used this inspiration to create change, not because of the company's leadership, but *in spite of it*.

So it wasn't surprising that his department managed to make great progress at one particularly notable point in time – when he ignored the state of the rest of the business and ploughed on regardless. His department succeeded, in part, because they weren't dragged into the mire and depression that plagued the rest of the business. It was because they were allowed to lead the innovations, the changes and the evolutions that were required to take their department's initiatives to a new level.

They didn't do it in isolation, though. They did it in consultation with people who had their ears to the ground, who were listening to what the market was telling them, and who could clearly articulate their customers' needs. The early success that they saw was, because they were collaborating with other leaders who, they later discovered, were *also* working *in spite of* their so-called leader's plans.

Over his time with the business he observed leader after leader leave the business because their opinions weren't valued, their initiatives were foiled and, for every step forward that they took, they were dragged back by two, four, or even six steps.

SIGNS OF BAD LEADERSHIP

What are some of the symptoms of bad leadership? What's the

proverbial canary in the coal mine? Here is a list of the symptoms he recalls observing at the time.

- Inspiring, intelligent and previously successful leaders left the business, or were pushed.
- Customers were unhappy (indeed, some key customers were starting to leave too).
- A pall of gloom and cynicism hung around the employees.
- Disparaging comments and speculation about the company's future were bandied around as if they were fact.
- The company had a mushroom culture.[v]
- The person in charge of the business's core product was unqualified for the position.
- Employees didn't seem to know what they were doing, why, or how it contributed towards a bigger picture or indeed what the bigger picture was.
- The company's ambitious growth targets were based on guesswork and hope, not fact.

The Secret Army in this business was struggling with a general who wasn't clear about the battle plan, and the strategy didn't seem to relate to the current terrain (external environment). In the meantime, the enemy (competitors) were winning the battle by providing a cheaper product that was easier to sell. Without clear differentiation about why this company's product was actually superior (which, in many respects it was – or had the potential to be), its future was doomed.

The irony is that the leader was neither an uncaring person, nor an unintelligent one. Yet something had gone horribly wrong and somehow, his efforts seemed to make things worse, not better.

It's ignorant to assume that any single key factor – including a leader who is not a leader – could be the single point of failure for any business. It's usually a combination of factors. However, the person who told me this story noticed one thing, specifically, that consistently let the business down: communication.

---

[v] See Chapter 10 for more on this subject.

MODELS OF COMMUNICATION: SPEAKING, LISTENING AND FEEDBACK

Any journalism or communications student will be able to tell you about communication models and their evolution over time. We've gone from the Shannon-Weaver model, which talks about information sources, encoders, channels and receivers (and which implies that those receiving messages are passively consuming the information that the sender encodes), to Wilbur Schramm's model, which takes into account the need to encode and decode the message (i.e. make sense of it) and includes 'noise' as a factor in disrupting the flow of information.[w] Then there's Vardaman's TRIM model[76] (target, receiver, impact and methods/media) and a dozen more besides.[77]

What these models don't do, however, is put communications in the context of leadership and business.

Communication is a two-way exchange. It involves both speaking and listening. Leaders need to understand the importance of listening to their employees more than anyone else. Being listened to makes a huge difference.

I'll never forget the power of a leader who entered my sphere of influence while I was at university. He was leading a department in the faculty of sciences. I'd done one course with the department and worked for them for a few days as a temporary assistant but, to him, it didn't seem to matter whether I was a student, a worker, or the Vice-Chancellor of the university. He gave me a gift I'll never forget.

One day, when I came in for a private appointment with him, he turned away from his computer and gave me his full attention. There was something intense about his gaze – not intense in a freaky, off-putting way, but intense in the way that I knew he was focused solely on the information I had to share with him. The rest of the world ceased to exist. There

---

[w] For a simple summary of these models and their evolution, take a look at http://www.yourarticlelibrary.com/advertising/communication-models-different-communication-models-as-proposed-by-many-management-theorists/22244/

was nothing in that room but my problem, the two of us, and the distant hope of a solution.

He had that indefinable 'charisma', unquestionably, but what he also did is give people one of the most valuable gifts of all: his full attention.

This next section is about people like him, not when they've risen to the leadership positions that they tend towards, but when they're sitting behind the scenes.

To find out who the real power behind the throne is, you need to find the person the decision-makers are listening to.

WHO ARE THE HIDDEN INFLUENCERS?

Earlier, we touched on 'guerrilla leaders' and the 'butterfly in a box' syndrome. These arise when hidden influencers are not listened to, and so take arms against the current leadership in frustration.

There's another way of looking at these people – as the movers and shakers inside an organisation that can take the seed of an idea and spread it until it germinates in their team or department or division. This is how to identify the hidden influencers.

These hidden influencers come in two groups:

- those who shape leaders' opinions, and
- those who shape teams' opinions.

When you're in a meeting room and someone asks a general question, who do people turn to first? Who's the one who gets the most glances for approval? Who's the one whose word is law? These are generally those in a position of power, the decision-makers. If they're not in the room and they're supposed to be, meetings are generally re-scheduled or cancelled.

In Western cultures, it's fairly easy to tell who the leaders are. In Eastern interactions, however, it's a whole different ballgame. There, it is often the second-in-command who does the speaking and the directing. The real leader may sit silently throughout the entire interaction. But when they *do* speak, their word is law.

Despite the vast differences between Eastern and Western cultures, this commonality exists: there is always a 'second-in-command' who shapes leaders' opinions. They're the ones who leaders will listen to. They may be high or low in the hierarchy, but their opinion matters almost more than anyone else's. And, more often than not, it isn't easy to tell who the hidden influencers are unless you observe what is *not being said* as much as what is.

SHAPING LEADERS' OPINIONS

One CEO I worked with was a hard man to convince. He required statistics and data to support even the simplest decision and, even then, he would often ignore the data if it didn't fit with his worldview. But he would always trust opinions from one individual within the business, let's call him Fred. If you were in a meeting where both the leader and his second-in-command were present, you could physically see the directions of decisions changing when Fred spoke. Something about Fred made the CEO pay attention in a way that no-one else could.

Interestingly, Fred didn't do so well with shaping teams' opinions. His sphere of influence was heavily weighted to get the CEO's ear. He had strong opinions, and these didn't always sit well with other departments. However, he had an undisputed power: the ear of the leader.

Have you ever watched the film *My Big Fat Greek Wedding*? In it, the Greek mother utters this wonderful line, 'The man, he is the head. But the woman, she is the neck. And the neck can turn the head any way she wants.'

Fred was the CEO's neck.

The trick for anyone in the organisation who couldn't reach the CEO but whose initiatives made sense, held up to scrutiny, and were good for the business, was to convince Fred. And if Fred was convinced the chances were that the CEO's reluctance would, almost mysteriously, disappear. Then it was simply up to the managers to convince their teams to get on board with the idea.

Which brings us to the next part of the equation: how do you shape teams' opinions?

SHAPING TEAMS' OPINIONS

It's a team's job to work with their leader, take instructions from them and execute actions. It's a leader's job to know when the instructions are too much for the team, not executable, or illogical. It's the team cheerleader's job to rally the crowd and encourage everyone to get on board. In some ways, the team cheerleader is just as important as the leader because they're more constant in the lives of the team members. They're physically present (not always away in meetings) and, more often than not, they possess an energy or enthusiasm that carries others through when team morale is low.

In ancient times, these cheerleaders may have been the army's drummers, storytellers, standard-bearers or buglers – someone who doesn't fight on the front lines, but whose role in keeping a team motivated is undisputed.

In many companies, these are the marketing teams. In others, HR fulfils the function. In some companies, teams take it upon themselves to alternate who takes the role of the cheerleader. And in great teams, if the cheerleader fails, other team members step up and inject their own cheer.

Cheerleaders can exist in almost any team. In many businesses these days, the nature of teams can be fluid or people often belong to more than one team, so it's important to identify – and use – the cheerleaders who can help other team members embrace a plan and encourage them to work towards its success.

Some of the best organisations I've worked with have clear reporting lines, clear team structures, clear goals and ways of assessing those goals, as well as encouraging others to meet those goals. They also have a fundamental understanding of human nature. They know that people play different roles in their lives, and they find ways to accommodate this.

For example, they (tacitly or explicitly) encourage teams to build and disband as and when they are required. Teams will be formed with those who work together, day in and day out. But teams can also be groups of employees who inspire each other.

Do you have the trusted advisors that you need?

Regardless of what position you occupy in a company, it's critical that you are able to work with or get inspiration from others, and that you have individuals available to listen to you, advise you, support you and exchange ideas with you.

It is often more difficult for leaders to find this support. There's a transition phase in every leader's life when they go beyond working and collaborating with their team in an entirely risk-free and open way, to where they have to withhold information – often for the team's own good.

Likewise, because leaders are required to show unwavering confidence, they often lack a sounding board that allows them to express their doubts or someone to pick them up when they're feeling down. That's why senior leadership teams exist, and are so powerful; and it's why leaders have hidden influencers – beyond the board, or parliament. These influencers are people they trust with their lives.

Leaders need advice too.

Truly successful organisations know this. That's why they build teams where leaders from other divisions can advise each other without fear of recrimination or of looking weak or indecisive in front of their employees. These networks may exist formally or informally – a group of people who play football or golf together after work, or a women's group that gets together to discuss what leadership means for them in what is (still) a largely male-dominated hierarchy.

They are the places where people feel 'safe' and safety is an essential element of successful teams. Everyone needs to feel safe.

Feeling safe at work not only allows us to keep going for longer, but it reduces stress levels, increases happiness, and improves productivity. Having safe places for idea exchange – so that we can listen to our own hidden influencers – isn't just a 'nice-to-have'. The hormones that our bodies release in safe environments actually keep us going. They're called endorphins, and commonly-known and understood ones include dopamine (otherwise known as the reward hormone), serotonin (the confidence hormone), oxytocin (the bonding hormone) and cortisol (the stress hormone).

Great teams allow people to feel 'safe', and in doing so enable them to build up essential levels of serotonin and other community-related hormones such as oxytocin. We need teams to be able to reduce the amount of the hormone cortisol – the opponent of serotonin. Cortisol is the stress-hormone. It is released when we enter 'fight or flight' mode.

Let's face it; most of our modern jobs induce large amounts of cortisol, which has been linked to chronic stress, digestive disorders, lower immune systems and even (yes, this is true!) an increased amount of fat around the belly.[78]

In conclusion, building up 'happy' teams isn't just good for the productivity of the teams, but it's actually good for their hearts, their bodies and their souls. Plus, incidentally, because they're 'safe', they are also free to explore riskier opportunities within the safety of their groups which can, in turn, become important initiatives for the business.

HOW DO YOU KNOW YOU'RE SAFE?

It's hard to know who to trust if you're in an environment that breeds distrust, but if you're in a circle of safety where everyone has each other's backs, everything changes. You trust people to tell you if you're going in the wrong direction. You trust people to do what needs to be done. You trust people to work together. You trust your team to deliver, to help others deliver and to help one another when times are tough.

You know you're safe when you trust people more than you doubt them, when they prove their loyalty time and again, and when you know that you can express your fears and concerns as easily as you can express your ideas and general thoughts.

This safety drives success.

Ultimately, perhaps this is what hidden influencers really give those they support: comfort, safety, a sense that people are 'like me', and reassurance that taking the lonely road of being a leader isn't always as lonely.

Regardless, it's an important lesson for all of us to take away – find your hidden influencers, use them, and be aware of who the hidden influencers are that can turn your leader's head, because they could help you help yourself and your team get sign-off more easily, and achieve even greater things.

> **LESSON 11:** Hidden influencers determine your army's strategy, and can even be more powerful than leaders. They are the 'neck' that turns the leaders' heads. Get them on board and your team will thrive.

Key Takeaways:

- *To find out who the real power behind the throne is, you need to identify the person the decision-makers are listening to.*

- *Hidden influencers come in two groups: those who shape leaders' opinions, and those who shape teams' opinions.*

- *Great companies build teams where people of relevant levels of seniority feel safe enough to speak openly and advise each other without fear of recrimination or of looking weak or indecisive in front of their employees.*

- *The safety of a supportive team releases endorphins such as dopamine, serotonin and oxytocin, which are responsible for people continuing to fight against the odds and achieve extraordinary feats – together.*

Chapter 13: Making Change Possible

How important is it to admit to failure? Why are trade-offs so important? Is there a simple, three-step formula for success? This chapter answers these questions. It talks about change agents and how fear can make or break change, using the example of a charity who helped people embrace new technology to do their expenses.

Imagine, for a moment, a business 'utopia'.

In this perfect world, all employees are happy, all company goals are achieved, everyone works together productively, all initiatives are robust and progressive, and everyone in the management-employee chain supports these initiatives wholeheartedly. In this utopia, all managers are brilliant, all employees are excellent, all leaders are strong, all boards are wise, and everyone earns what they deserve and goes home feeling fulfilled and believing their lives are full of meaning.

We live in the real world, though, and in this world no company is perfect; they all have their own strengths and weaknesses.

That's why the SWOT[x] analysis was created.[79] It's a quick yet thorough way of critically assessing a company's strengths and weaknesses, as well as the opportunities and threats facing it.

Unfortunately, admitting our weaknesses is hard – for both businesses and individuals.

Great companies – and great leaders within those companies – however, know that tools like the SWOT analysis are helpful. These companies embrace the ability to look 'beneath their skin' and find areas of weakness because they know that wherever there's weakness, there's room for improvement. They're not satisfied with just being average.

---

[x] SWOT is an acronym for *strengths, weaknesses, opportunities* and *threats*. Some authors credit SWOT to Albert S. Humphrey, who led a convention at the Stanford Research Institute (now SRI International) in the 1960s and 1970s using data from Fortune 500 companies. However, Humphrey himself did not claim the creation of SWOT, and the origins remain obscure.

They're self-critical and, arguably more importantly, they know that it's worth taking the time to look inward. Great companies reflect on what needs to be improved, decide what actions should be taken in order to make these changes, and do it. But even the best companies come unstuck when they try to do too much all at once.

When everyone tries to achieve everything without a clear sense of where they are going and why, things fall apart. Without clarity, it's difficult to row together in the same direction. Without a coherent sense of purpose, even the best teams can find themselves competing against each other. Without purpose, everyone does what Dory does in *Finding Nemo*: they 'just keep swimming'– but not in the same direction. And when everyone is trying to achieve different things without an overarching strategy, it's like a rowing four all trying to pull their oars at slightly different times. Confusion reigns, and no-one's going to win any medals. In fact, they're barely likely to get off the starting line.

We need to make choices, and then try to change, based on the best outcomes. However, in order to head towards that business utopia, our leaders have to make difficult, often unpopular, decisions – enter the trade-off.

THE IMPORTANCE OF THE TRADE-OFF

Great companies and great leaders have learned (no matter how difficult it seems, at times) to make a trade-off between what 'has to be' done and what 'should be' done.

Greg McKeown, author of *Essentialism*,[80] puts it this way: 'As painful as they can sometimes be, trade-offs represent a significant opportunity. By forcing us to weigh both options and strategically select the best one for us, we significantly increase our chance of achieving the outcome we want.'

Trade-offs are about making decisions, often hard decisions, about what to remain focused on and what to let go. In a world with so many options available to us, having to make a decision from so many options can sometimes seem overwhelming. But choices are particularly necessary in business for three reasons.

- Employees need direction.
- Focus breeds success.
- Having choices already made for us makes sticking to a path much easier.

Then, once choices have been made, some things will inevitably have to change.

The book *The Naked Leader*[81] was published in 2002. In the fifteen years since its publication, one core element has stuck with me. David Taylor created a formula for success that is so fundamental it almost seems obvious. He proposes, quite simply, that there is one sure-fire way to achieve success: follow these four sequential steps.

1. Know where you want to go.
2. Know where you are now.
3. Know what you have to do to get to where you want to go.
4. Do it!

In business, once the 'looking inwards' has taken place (know where you are now) and the decision has been made about which trade-offs to choose (know what you have to do to get what you want), the time comes to set people on that path towards evolution (do it – make the change). Change isn't always comfortable but, as George Bernard Shaw said, 'Progress is impossible without change.'

A business set on making change happen has two choices:

- to force change on people, or
- to lead them towards change.

We'll assume that since you've read this far you're not the kind of person who believes in forcing change on people. Therefore, in order to lead your employees towards change, you'll need help in the form of change agents and then you'll need to remind change-resistant people that they're better at coping with change than they may think!

CHANGE AGENTS

These change agents come in a variety of forms. We've already spoken about frustrated storytellers, undiscovered idea-generators and hidden influencers who can respectively find stories, unearth insights and steer leaders towards a certain direction. Now we'll look at the change-makers and those they will interact with: the challengers, the cheerleaders and the silent assassins.[82]

Challengers do what you'd expect – they challenge the need for change. They ask questions like, 'Why should we change? This is the way we've always done it.' They may be loud about their objections but, with logic and time, they'll usually come around with the help of cheerleaders.

Cheerleaders are the champions of change. They may not always be 'cheerful' but they're certainly committed to change and prepared to be vociferous about the need for change and its benefits. They'll try to bring the challengers on-side. They have a tough job, however, because although the challengers may be difficult to bring around, they're not nearly as difficult to convince as the silent assassins.

Silent assassins are sceptics who will object, just not vocally. They'll just ignore the need for change and carry on doing what they've always done. They may even further sabotage your efforts, surreptitiously.

CHANGE AND FEAR

So how do companies help their employees to *want* to change, or at least not fear it? They make best use of the tools in their arsenal: the people who see the need for change and or embrace it; and the scenarios that are familiar to those who have already gone through change in the past.

The flippant statement 'we all fear change' is not true. Some personality types love change, they thrive on it, and they're at their best when they're being faced by a challenge that needs to be overcome. Without change or challenge these types get bored and look for something else to occupy their time.

However, even those who hate or fear change go through it more often than they suspect. Getting married, changing jobs, moving house, having a child: all of these involve massive change and yet as humans we enjoy (or at least, tolerate) these kinds of change and take them in our stride. If people really were afraid of change, no-one would ever buy a new car or go for a job promotion. Indeed, 'People don't fear change. They fear change being forced on them if they have no say or control'.[83]

Alternatively, people may not actually fear the 'change' itself'; they may merely be resisting the concept of change because it actually brings out one of our five basic human fears: fear of extinction, mutilation, loss of autonomy, separation, or ego-death.[84] In other words, the fear that we could die, be injured, lose our ability to act independently, be separated from the ones we love, or lose our identity. We're not usually aware of these basic human fears, as they lurk in the dark places behind our conscious minds, but if these fears exist, as psychologists believe they do, change can be threatening precisely because it's forcing us to confront something that we don't even know exists! Logically, therefore, if change is too threatening – either consciously *or* subconsciously – it's hardly surprising that people show resistance to it.

So how do we build the case for change and bring people along with us? Authors Chip and Dan Heath have a suggestion. In their book *Switch: how to change things when change is hard*,[85] they set out a remarkably simple, eloquently articulated path for change. To summarise it here is not to do it justice – it's worth reading the book yourself to discover their examples – but here follows a summary.

For them, change is about elephants, riders and a path. Using an analogy they discovered in *The Happiness Hypothesis* by Jonathan Haidt, they explain how change is about getting the elephant (our emotional side) and the rider (our rational side) to go down the same path together, without trying to pull in different directions.

Here's how they explain the process.

To begin, it's worth noting that sometimes people resist change if they simply don't know what to do. Their first solution is to direct our rational 'rider' by identifying bright spots – examples of success that can be duplicated or extended to other parts of the business. Another solution is to make sure that the goal is clear (i.e. if people need to understand *why* they need to change).

Secondly, they talk about motivating the elephant – i.e. helping people move towards change emotionally. One way to do this is to make things 'real' for people by putting it into a tangible context – for example, explaining how much money is being lost by dumping a basket of ball-bearings on the floor, or showing how much of a difference people are making by putting a tick on a board every time something is completed. They also recommend 'shrinking the change' or 'growing your people' to help encourage emotional engagement.

Lastly, they talk about shaping the path down which everyone involved in the change must travel. One way to do this effectively is to change the context in which people act, so they can't rely on old habits. This, in turn, forces people to change their habits by requiring them to build new ones that are more aligned with the desired behaviour. Another way is to 'rally the herd'. Their book includes some fantastic examples about how to make desired behaviour contagious. [86]

AN EXAMPLE: SUBMITTING EXPENSES ONLINE

Here's an example that should be easy for most business people to understand if they've ever travelled for business and had to be reimbursed for the cost of their transport, accommodation or meals.

Imagine that your business is moving from doing the expenses submission process manually to automating it. Your employees have two choices: they can change to adapt and use the new system, incorporate it into a better way of working and ultimately be more productive, or they can resist it, keep doing things the way they've always been done and ultimately either become extremely frustrated or possibly even suffer dire consequences (in this case, not get their expenses paid – ever).

How do managers, stuck between needing to improve efficiency (and ultimately profits) and the desire to protect and support their employees reconcile this, and use the philosophy of elephant, rider and path to help them make that change?

The customer of a company I once worked for did this brilliantly.[87] These are the challenges they were up against, and how they made it work.

You'd think that it would be easy to encourage people to use a system if it means they'll get their money back sooner. After all, rationally, it's better to be reimbursed sooner. You'd think that they would want to use a system that lets them do their expenses online, even via their mobile phone with an app. Again, rationally, it's better if you don't have to worry about losing a receipt because you've already taken a photo of it and submitted it, and you don't need to think about it beyond that.

But ease of use and speed of payment wasn't enough to help some employees in this company make the change. Some of them found it too inconvenient to use a new system. Some were used to having special dispensations given when they lost a receipt. Some even liked getting a great big wodge of cash when they submitted their expenses once a year. Some had built special macros into their spreadsheets to make their own processes easier. Some just liked doing it the way they had always done it.

How did this business solve the problem?

To put it simply: they started by getting the emotional and the rational parts of their employees' brains aligned.

As a charity, they were used to working with people who weren't particularly technologically advanced, and they were really worried about having to adopt new technology. So they took a three-step process.

- Initially, they created 'bright spots' – they engaged storytellers who had tried the software as part of an initial 'rollout programme' and loved it. These individuals became their new product adoption advocates. They raved about the new software – how easy it was to use, how quickly they were reimbursed, how 'un-scary' it really was.
- Then the company set up training sessions for every single eligible employee – if they needed it – and, here's the brilliant part, it was run by the product adoption advocates (storytellers) themselves. The company also provided explanatory documents for those who didn't want hands-on training.
- And then they did something quite dramatic: they set a deadline for using the new software. And they enforced that deadline. Of course, people who had real problems were still paid back eventually (but they didn't know that at the time).

Soon, the new software was adopted by almost the entire company.

There's only one more group of critical people involved in this change who we haven't discussed yet – the accounting teams who processed the expenses. The reason why we've left them to last is because, although processing expenses online was a whole new way of working for them, which required them to change working practices and adapt, this group was actually the first to come on-side. They managed to learn how to use the new software quickly because it made good sense to them: they could see the benefits of using it, and they knew *why* the change was necessary.

This company predicted resistance, informed people, inspired them, set and enforced deadlines – and managed to change behaviour entirely in a technology-averse industry.

THE REASONS BEHIND CHANGE

Adopting expenses software worked for the finance team because they knew why it had to happen in the first place, early on. Only occasionally is it simply not possible to explain the need for change (i.e. the company is cutting costs because, if they don't, they'll go out of business). In almost every other instance, it's far easier in the long run if companies are as open and honest about the need for change as possible.

Even if employees don't see the need for change, disagree with the reasons for change or believe that other options would be better, consultancy is a critical part of any successful change initiative: explain, try to bring people on board, and then make it inevitable.

However, as Frederick Douglass says, 'If there is no struggle, there is no progress'.[88] Sometimes it feels like anything that is worth achieving must require struggle and pain, and particularly when massive change is taking place – but that's not necessarily true. Sometimes making change a reality requires small, consistent tweaks, done by many, many people together, to create a whole new amazing future. When people work together towards a single purpose and when they know where they're going, why, and how to get there, change is almost inevitable.

> **LESSON 12:** Your Secret Army wants to do better if they can understand why it's worth doing. Help them get there – plan for change, lead it, and use your cheerleaders to help you.

Key Takeaways:

- *Great companies embrace the ability to look 'beneath their skin' and find areas of weakness, because they know that wherever there's weakness, there's room for improvement.*

- *Hard decisions need to be made about what to remain focused on and what to let go – and trade-offs have to be balanced.*

- *Change isn't always comfortable but, as George Bernard Shaw said, 'Progress is impossible without change.'*

- *Look out for helpful change agents. Their support can ease the change process significantly.*

Chapter 14: Relationships and Chameleons

Why are some people such a pain in the butt to work with while others, almost unknowingly, build successful teams and inspire others? We answer this question while addressing the importance of attitude, collaboration, and the need to understand why the us/them mentality exists. We introduce the concept of pre-competing, and talk about how to be a team chameleon. We end with eighteen tips for brilliant relationship-building at work.

When I was younger, I was extremely stubborn. Hardly anyone could convince me to do something I didn't want to do. And if I simply *had* to do something (like clean my room or unpack the dishwasher), I would end up doing it with bad grace.

Some employees are like that too. In my experience, it often happens in circumstances like these.

- If they have been in the business longer than others, and think they know more about 'the way things are done around here'.
- If they have seen things that have been tried before, and failed before.
- If they feel like they're unappreciated or not listened to (so they give out advice grudgingly, fully expecting that they'll be ignored anyway).
- If they really would rather be doing something else – at another company, in another job, or in another city/country/world.
- If they have an overly high opinion of themselves.
- If they are defensive when asked to explain their actions.
- If they think that there's a better way to do it.
- If they don't understand why they have to do it.
- If they just don't want to do it, plain and simple.

I've worked with people like this in the past, and I've taken two approaches with them. The first approach was to listen to them, coach them, encourage them, help them in areas of weaknesses, and help them realise their strengths and develop them. It was exhausting, although in many ways worth it.

Then there's the second approach, which is to realise that, despite any or all the efforts you've put in, they simply aren't going to ever want to do the job for which they are being paid. Sometimes it's possible to realise this before you've put the effort in but sooner or later the decision is reached that it's simply time for them to move on. It's great if they can be encouraged to move on to a role they *do* want to play, but sometimes employers just have to take on that painful, unpopular and soul-destroying task of 'performance management'.

In some instances, performance management can actually be a good way of encouraging behaviour change and, with the right coaching, people can actually realise what behaviours are preventing them from working effectively with others and make the effort to improve. Sometimes these previously under-performing individuals can rise to the challenge and excel – and all it took was a bit of discipline, guidance and self-awareness. In other instances, performance management is just 'management speak' for waiting long enough for someone to resign, or going through enough steps so they can be fired.

IT'S ALL ABOUT ATTITUDE

Fortunately, the vast majority of employees are not like I was as a teenager, or like those we've just discussed above. Instead, they are hard-working and appropriately intelligent for their role. They realise that a job takes up most of their waking hours, and it's worth enjoying the job and being fulfilled while doing it, but they're also pragmatic enough to realise that a job is just that – a job – not a life.

Regardless of how people approach work, it is their attitude when working with others that either creates conflict or the capacity for greatness. No-one is ever going to agree with everyone else all of the time. In fact, while I'm not a management coach or a marriage counsellor (although I've done elements of both roles in my time), I know that it's human nature for disagreement to exist as long as there is more than one brain in a room. When disagreements get to a point where neither party is prepared to budge from their position, something or someone needs to be able to break the deadlock.

When two parties can't see eye-to-eye, they're hardly likely to want to collaborate. There's an art to encouraging them to budge far enough that they can both get a bit of what they want, and both ending up feeling like they haven't lost. It's an art that requires the patience of Jude, the wisdom of Solomon, and the thick skin of many politicians.

Without a way to compromise, marriages would never work, wars will never cease, and businesses will never move forward. So, like it or not, we often have to work with people who think differently to us, who believe (stubbornly) that they are right when we (stubbornly) think that our way is the only way to do things. We have to collaborate in order to get things done.

COLLABORATION

Effective collaboration begins by understanding that people are people. They have hopes, fears, dreams and frustrations. They have mood swings and irrational phobias. You can never truly know or try to understand them all and they're influenced by more factors in more diverse and complex ways than any of us can begin to comprehend. People are all at different stages of their lives and want different things (or perhaps may not even know what they want and are waiting for 'it' to turn up).

What a Secret Army of individuals within a workplace can do, however, is provide and enhance a shared sense of purpose, a common goal, a feeling of achieving something that is greater than the sum of its parts. That's what makes a team, creates a tribe, and makes an initiative worth doing. And that is often the core of compromise – a realisation that there are many ways to reach a goal and that as long as they're moving forwards rather than backwards, sometimes one party will win, sometimes another one will triumph, and sometimes the answer will be a solution that no-one really loves but no-one really hates either.

It's called compromise. Get used to it.

But we take our roles very seriously, and any actions that undermine our perceived value of self can be hurtful, far beyond the intended (or unintended) affront to our abilities. It's because, no matter whether we live for our jobs or do a job in order to live, we identify ourselves with our profession. It's almost inevitable, when you think about it, because we spend more of our waking lives in job-related tasks than we do with our loved ones. Sad, but true.

So when we're in work positions that put us in opposition to each other, we're not just fighting for the right to be right on whatever point of contention is debatable. We're actually fighting for our very identities.

WORKPLACE CONFLICTS, IDENTITY AND HUMAN EVOLUTION

As humans, we've had to make decisions ever since we first started evolving. We've had to identify whether threats were things we should eat / run away from / have intercourse with. Our primal brains are primed to identify threats or collaborators. Indeed, if you believe the evidence put forward by Matthew D. Lieberman of *Social: Why Our Brains Are Wired to Connect*[89] (which we covered in Chapter 10), then you will know that FMRI scans show that the 'human connections' part of our brain is active *even when we are resting*. Connecting and making sense of our world, it seems, is our default human state.

So, when we first meet someone new and we ask the question 'What do you do?', our purpose isn't just to find out more about them or start a polite conversation. Actually, the answer to this seemingly innocuous phrase allows us to put people in boxes, to define them, and to make sense of their place in the world as well as ours. If their answer is interesting to us, we decide to accept them or collaborate with them, for now.

It makes sense from an evolutionary perspective too. We gain benefits from being in groups of people. It's easier to hunt, defend ourselves and raise offspring in a group. This evolutionary advantage has led us to crave the need for social connection. It's why we have a tendency to form groups and it's why people are happier when they're part of a group, supported by others with similar goals or interests to their own. Moreover, it's also why we see 'others' (anyone who is not part of our group, culture or team) as a potential threat.

As leaders of a Secret Army of employees and supporters (including customers and suppliers), it's our job to find and use those hidden connections or, if they aren't there already, to create them.

BREAKING DOWN THE US/THEM MENTALITY

Have you ever worked in a company where people sat in siloes, doing their own thing? If so, you're likely to have noticed an us/them mentality that clearly defined different teams. It's natural – people form groups and sometimes the very thing that creates a group is having something to work against (an opposition or 'enemy').

In fact, the very nature of group dynamics is quite curious, in and of itself. If you put people into opposing teams, something strange happens: new allegiances form, old connections are ignored, and those who 'cross the party lines' are frowned upon. It even happens at the company picnic and sports day, one of those great (I use the word 'great' ironically – I'm not much of a fan of 'organised fun') initiatives designed to foster intra-company collaboration. The idea behind an organised fun day is to get people from all walks of life, from all parts of the business and with a variety of skills, salaries and interests, to miraculously come together and get to know each other in 'friendly' competitive sports that allow them to create new teams and break down existing barriers.

It works for some people. It's a huge failure for others. What it does do, however, is clearly demonstrate that some teams manage to form bonds quickly and successfully, and create success. They go through the 'forming, storming, norming, performing' phases of team-building extremely quickly – in less than a day – in order to be able to achieve a series of goals. Admittedly, these goals are often arbitrary and usually prove nothing more than that someone has great skill at balancing on a beam, running with a stick, or dressing up as a sumo wrestler. So, what happens with these teams that *are* successful in such a short space of time? What do they do differently? To answer this question, we'll look at an example of one leader who, during my interactions with her, was almost always successful.

What's her secret? Pre-competing.

CAN 'ORGANISED FUN' ACTUALLY WORK TO BUILD TEAMS? THE SECRET OF PRE-COMPETING

I had a colleague who was great fun. Vivacious and determined, a natural leader, a fantastic sportswoman and incredibly competitive. If you gave her an objective and threw her in a room with a team of people, they would usually look to her for instruction before turning to others of a similar status. I don't think she even thought about it; she just led. It was instinctive.

Curiously – and it seemed unrelated at the time – she almost always ended up on the winning team at sports events, company 'fun days' or competitive activities of any sort. You might think it is coincidence, or her own innate competitiveness that propelled her teams to success, but I'm convinced that wasn't the whole story.

Almost unerringly, she would find her way onto a team of like-minded individuals at these company events. I never asked her if she 'jigged' the teams or pulled strings so that she would deliberately be teamed up with other competitive athletes. In fact, I suspect that something more fundamental was taking place behind the scenes. She was pre-competing.

By pre-competing, I mean that she was working to get the odds in her favour long before the competition really began. Sometimes she did it consciously. Often, I don't think she was even aware of doing it.

How did she do it?

Firstly, she had a very strong network of connections. And these like-minded individuals were pre-competing too. Like her, they were also leveraging opportunities and finding ways of setting things up so that events worked in their favour long before the fun-day's teams were ever announced.

Although she never broke any explicit guidelines, she wasn't 'playing by the rules', because both she and the similarly tenacious, competitive leaders who she aligned herself with were instinctively exploiting the hidden advantages of collaboration long before things were made official. She was doing what leaders have done since time immemorial, since long before Sun Tzu wrote *The Art of War*, which is quite literally the handbook on strategy. She was doing covert reconnaissance: examining the battlefield for hidden advantages, investigating her opponents and building a strategy that would put her, and her chosen army, in the most strategically advantageous position before the war commenced.

More often than not (almost always, in fact), her team won.

Obviously, it was great to be on her team. Yes, it's nice to win, there's no question about that, and the likelihood of winning certainly attracted more people to want to be part of her team. This, in turn, gave her a bigger pool of 'top athletes' to draw from which, logically, made her teams stronger. But it was more than that. Not only did her innate desire to win propel her forward, and her grasp of competitive analysis and planning give her and her team a strategic advantage; arguably more importantly, she made everyone feel like they had something valuable to add. And they did, because as she prepared her strategy (whether it was for tackling a certain project or winning at laser-tag), she actively chose the people she wanted to work with, plotted each team member's weaknesses and strengths, and found ways to leverage their strengths and use other team members' strengths to mitigate any weaknesses.

The irony is, she didn't consider herself a leader. Yet her actions are almost written into the leadership handbook.

Of course, she saw results.

What was interesting, however, is how she was perceived by groups and individuals who weren't part of her carefully selected group. They resented her. To be fair, she expected a high return from her team members, and it wasn't always fun to be part of the team in the preparation process. In addition, since no-one is perfect, it's also fair to point out that she didn't play well with others who weren't prepared to put in the same amount of effort as her, or those who rode the coat-tails of the hard work she and her team had accomplished. Her great ability to create a team made non-team-members feel ever so slightly resentful of the fact that they weren't 'part of the gang'… until they were.

The funny thing was that she was also a team chameleon. As soon as the boundaries or definition of the team changed, she became a different type of team member; not always a leader, but always as vivacious and determined and tenacious. She could hop from team to team, dipping in and out, and building relationships as required. It mystified her old teammates, and probably made them feel a bit lonely or left out when they were no longer part of the 'in-crowd', but because she also had an uncanny ability to retain relationships with the power-makers in teams where she had been a member in the past, she could also leverage those relationships when required. And in so doing, she was able to leverage intra-company connections to transcend barriers of team, role, responsibility or even country.

LESSONS FOR INTRA-COMPANY CONNECTIONS: HOW TO BE A TEAM CHAMELEON

In our interconnected world, it's no longer enough to form lasting team alliances. Like my colleague, we have to be team chameleons. We might have been able to work quite comfortably in business siloes once, but our world is now too complex, too interconnected and too demanding for us to only gain expertise in one area or work in one group.

It's human nature to form groups and exclude others. It's also human nature to collaborate with people 'like us'. So it's natural to want to work with those who share common interests and/or skills. Marketers build relationships with marketers. Salespeople work with salespeople. Developers trust developers, etc. We like to hang out with those with whom we have things in common. But, as a consequence, those who are not part of our team fall outside of our 'circle of safety' and, as such, are treated as enemies or, at minimum, ignored.

This is very bad for companies.

My colleague, however, managed to build new circles of safety every time she became a member of a new team. This is what she did, almost without thinking.

- Identify a clear goal (win at ten pin bowling or launch a radio advertising campaign, it didn't matter).
- Pick a team.
- Identify the team's strengths and weaknesses.
- Allocate people tasks at which they're likely to excel.
- Create a plan.
- Pre-identify barriers to success and build those into a plan, along with ways to overcome them.
- Constantly analyse success during the process, looking for opportunities for improvement and weak spots.
- Set people clear, achievable goals with firm deadlines.
- Plan for those deadlines to be over-run and build in a buffer beforehand.
- Remind people what success looks like.
- Act as a lynch-pin for the activity, keeping on top of all the moving parts.
- Keep the goal firmly in mind.
- Push people when they need pushing, taking on tasks if they're not likely to be achieved in time and will let down the entire team or project.
- Pull all the moving parts together for the final push.
- Get the project delivered.
- Celebrate success.
- Identify room for improvement for the future.

Really, it's Project Management 101.

What was fascinating about the way she did it, though, is that she was able to apply these project management fundamentals to every single work-based (and life-based) activity. And the result was almost inevitably success.

The other aspect of what she did was the more subconscious part, the part that pulled things together.

It's all very well producing a plan, sticking to the plan, making adjustments where necessary and pulling it all together at the end. The question is, will people still want to speak to you once the project is over?

For some people I've worked with, who have organised the most amazing events that won companies deals worth millions of pounds and had huge success ratings, the answer is a resounding 'no', simply because working with them was so incredibly unpleasant. One person with whom I worked was a truly brilliant event organiser, a lovely person, and one of the most unpleasant people to work with. The event he was responsible for running, innocuously named 'Foundation', became known anecdotally as 'The F-word' because its organiser was such a dictator.

So, what was the difference between these two organisers that made the one such a pleasure to work with, and the other such a chore? What did they do differently?

Here's a summary of their approaches.

Organiser 1 The leader and winner	Organiser 2 The 'F-word'
Connected with people.	Alienated people.
Wanted to work collaboratively, empowered people to win at their own tasks.	Pulled people in for isolated tasks, then discarded them.
Expected people to succeed, but be human and make mistakes.	Expected people to fail, had stringent deadlines and shouted to achieve results.
Worked with people.	Used people.
Task-oriented *and* people-oriented.	Task-oriented.

Focused on getting it done.	Focused on getting it perfect.
Expected everyone to work together.	Expected everyone to pull apart.
Guiding, but relaxed.	A control freak.
Multi-tasked comfortably.	Focused on only one task at a time.
Saw the task as a piece of something bigger.	Saw the task as a single goal and the end of the task as a finite state.

When tabulated like this, the real difference between the two approaches is obvious: one organiser pulled people together, the other pulled people apart. One gave people a sense that *they* were responsible for achieving something together, the other insisted that *he* was responsible for the project. The biggest difference was that the leader who didn't see herself as a leader actually was one, in her heart and soul. The other leader craved leadership, respect, acknowledgement and success and, ironically, that made him far less of a leader and more of a dictator.[y]

There's one other thing that was different about the organiser and leader who pre-competed; she had charisma. That may be a considerable, almost critical, element of her success. Unquestionably, her charisma helped her build relationships. But building relationships at work is not a specific, unique skill. Nor is it a secret art. It can be learned.

Any member of your Secret Army can use the pointers listed below to start building relationships that foster collaboration, both now and in the future.

---

[y] Is there a lesson here for world leaders? Perhaps we should have a 'hug a dictator' day? Perhaps this would give those pushy, inflexible, dictatorial types the recognition they crave, and make them feel less alienated, and alienate people less as a result.

EIGHTEEN TIPS FOR RELATIONSHIP-BUILDING AT WORK[z]

1. Be genuinely interested in people.
2. Ask questions.
3. Find out what people do on a daily basis.
4. Find out about their projects (in work) and life-interests (beyond work).
5. Figure out how you can work together and where your projects overlap.
6. Get invitations to meetings with teams you normally wouldn't work with, but where there's a logical overlap between what your teams do.
7. Attend all the 'lunch and learn' sessions your company offers, take all the free training you can get, and ask questions that help you understand the bigger picture.
8. Ignore people who tell you not to talk to others because 'they're not relevant' or 'they're not really on board', and broaden your understanding of the business (without getting bogged down in the details).
9. Make a point of talking to people who are leaving the business because once they're gone, you won't be able to get any more information from them. If they're deeply dissatisfied, then, obviously, take what they have to say with a pinch of salt, but listen anyway – there might be things you can learn or even fix.
10. Have coffee with people. Introduce yourself. Find out about their lives and families and what they did on the weekend. Remember this information and refer to it when you next see them.
11. Remember people's names. It's a very important way of connecting with them, and will stand you in good stead later.
12. Ask people for help – no matter whom, no matter where. (Obviously, check that they have the time or capacity to help you too).

---

[z] This list is inspired by Richard Templar's book, The Rules of Life: A personal code for living a better, happier, more successful kind of life. FT Press. 2015

13. Have lunch. This is important. Eating lunch in the office canteen or kitchen or wherever people 'hang out' in the office is very important. Eating together breaks down barriers between people. Avoid munching your sandwich while staring at your computer screen. It might save you a few minutes, but you'll lose the opportunity to build important networks.

14. Go to work-based social events. Personally, I'm not a huge fan of organised fun and often the hassle of getting home after a boozy night out with colleagues isn't very appealing. But the relationships you build with people when the barriers are down forge strong connections that cannot be denied.

15. Ask how *you* can help *them*. Find interesting ways of bringing your departments together.

16. Ask for their opinions. For example, if their department designs the widgets that become part of a tool that becomes part of a car, and you market that car, you still do have stuff in common, and it's worth listening to them. If you know how the widget works and why it's a much better widget than your competitors, listening to the widget-maker could, perhaps, be the secret to unlocking your next marketing campaign.

17. Share your team's successes outside of your team. You may not think that your HR department will care about the latest 'hack day' that your R&D team has organised, but actually, it could become a way to promote innovative working practices to potential new employees they are trying to recruit.

18. Always be polite. No matter how horrible your commute was, how hard it was to get your kids out of bed this morning, or the fact that you spilled coffee down your shirt, your colleagues don't deserve to have you take your frustrations out on them. Of course we're all human and have a right to complain, but if you can't find something nice to say sometimes,

it's better to say nothing at all – and to ask them how they are, instead.[90]

By using these fundamentally human skills for connecting with people, you'll find that building intra-company relationships is far easier than you think. And these bridges that you build over coffee will pay dividends later.

> **LESSON 13:** Don't let an 'us/them' mentality invade your Secret Army. Breaking down barriers helps us be more human. Collaborating with others helps to build success.

Key Takeaways:

- *A Secret Army within a workplace can provide and enhance a shared sense of purpose, a common goal, a feeling of achieving something that is greater than the sum of its parts. That's what makes a team, that's what creates a tribe, that's what makes an initiative worth doing.*

- *As leaders of a Secret Army of employees and supporters (including customers and suppliers), it's our job to find and use those hidden connections or, if they aren't there already, to create them.*

- *Inspirational leaders pre-compete. They work with other powerful individuals to get the odds in their favour long before the competition begins.*

- *Team chameleons are able to leverage intra-company connections in order to transcend barriers of team, role, responsibility or even country.*

SECTION 5

MARKETERS AND SALESPEOPLE – THE LOVERS AND THE FIGHTERS

Chapter 15: The Marketing Striptease

Want to know about the marketing striptease? We reveal all... We also talk about how anticipation can engage and persuade both employees and prospects; and how to make people buy your stuff because they want to, not because you told them to buy it. We discuss some great adverts (and why they work), talk about marketing campaigns and amplification, and uncover the logic behind social selling success.

This is not just a book about marketing. It's about management, leadership and the hidden power of your employees and your brand advocates. But marketing, leadership and sales actually have one very important element in common that drives success: knowing how to persuade others. Indeed, as we will cover in Chapter 17, we are *all salespeople.* In fact, the renowned author Daniel Pink wrote a book on the subject, called *To Sell is Human.*[91]

Like salespeople and leaders, marketers also have to be persuasive.

Not all the time. Not in a cringe-y way. And definitely not in a disingenuous way (those days have passed, now that we live in an era of authenticity, as we covered in Chapter 3 and again in Chapter 8). But marketers do have a very important job to do in order to convince perfect strangers to be aware of (and buy in to) their product or service category. The lessons marketers learn, and apply, every single day of their careers can help any leader, manager or influencer who needs to 'sell' something – whether that is an idea, a product or an initiative.

What marketers do is build layers of information that help reveal the correct level of detail their customers are looking for at the right time, in the right place, and in the right way.

Or do they?

Actually, the art of being a marketer isn't about building the layers of information – it's about taking them away. It's about revealing a little bit more tantalising information each time you engage with a prospective customer – I call it the marketing striptease.[92]

WHY DO PEOPLE WATCH A BURLESQUE SHOW?

Ever since the film *Burlesque*, featuring Cher and Christina Aguilera, re-popularised (and, arguably, de-stigmatised) the art form, places like Circus, Cellar Door and Proud Cabaret have opened their doors to men and women of all sexual preferences. At these popular venues, people go to eat, drink, and watch ladies remove their clothes in perfectly socially acceptable circumstances.[93]

What makes burlesque intriguing is not actually the naked ladies though. It's the journey, the tease of the strip, the 'what comes next' factor. That's what keeps the audience on the edge of their seats.

But when it comes to the art of persuasion in business, marketers are so eager to tell people why they should buy their stuff that they've forgotten what temptresses have known since time immemorial, and Amazon succeeds in doing with pre-release orders...

Sometimes having to wait for it makes you want it more. In our frantic, modern lives, we are so busy that we expect instant results. The same applies for content (the persuasive materials marketers produce in order to encourage people to buy) – it must hit our needs immediately, or it will be discarded. But marketers can learn from the mystery of the tease because people still like to be entertained... wooed... tantalised...

ANTICI... PATION

Frankie from *The Rocky Horror Picture Show* knew all about it. There is an art, as well as a science, to making people want to buy in to what you have to give them. If we want people to be really excited about whatever it is we have to sell, the art lies in the build-up. This means that marketers should aim to encourage people to read marketing messages in digestible chunks – revealing a new level of interest or insight as the form of content gets longer – so that, by the time the reader actually downloads something as meaty (or at least, as long-form) as an e-book or white paper, they're excited about it.

They've been taken on a journey towards downloading this content. And the destination is even sweeter as a result.

The same applies for the people in our teams, whether we realise it or not. They're not going to buy in to an idea the first time they hear about it. Perhaps some of them will – the raving fans, the cheerleaders, and those who immediately see the benefit of it – but the rest will take time and evidence to be convinced.

They too need to be wooed.

ANTICIPATION IN CONTENT MARKETING

What can marketers and leaders learn from burlesque? Quite simply, the art of intrigue, of building enthusiasm, is knowing how to reveal each piece of information in a digestible chunk that builds anticipation for what's next.

I compare the striptease theory of content revelation to the length of the skirt.

A tweet is an ankle-length skirt. Not much revealed, but it can be 'sexy' in and of itself (ask someone from 1820 about the sultriness of a 'well-turned' ankle and they'll tell you – phwoar!).

By the time you get to a knee-length skirt, you're in blog territory. You've got an idea of what the legs look like, but it's not really going to make you want to take the wearer out to dinner just yet (or buy the product immediately).

But when you get to thigh-high content (an e-book or white paper, or anything that requires their attention for more than ten minutes), you're talking serious value. It has to be good enough for your reader to be prepared to slip that digital £20 into your virtual garter belt. (I'm talking about giving up their details in order to download a white paper. What were you thinking?)

Not only are your readers going to expect enough value to give you their details, they also expect that the piece of content you produce will be worth their time. The chances are that your e-book or white paper will be at least 6-8 pages long (some are even 40-50 pages!), so, in order for people to read it – even to skim-read it – they'll need to save the PDF, add it to a digital reader tool of some sort or even print it out. Then you're asking a lot of their time and attention to skim it, picking out the bits that are interesting and ignoring the rest, never mind expecting them to read the whole document all the way through.

This means that you need to deliver on what you promise. If it's supposed to be a 'quick-read', don't make it onerous to digest. If it's supposed to be interesting, make sure it is!

ANTICIPATION FOR EMPLOYEES

The same applies to sharing information with employees. When a new initiative is announced, it needs to be explained properly.

These days, employees expect to get something from their companies *beyond* just a salary. These great expectations arise every time a new project, set of goals or corporate strategy is announced. It is the job of marketers, leaders and influencers across the business to entice people enough to get them to buy in to the initiative so that they're more likely to deliver the desired results.

Leaders may do this either by helping them see the bigger picture or by helping them realise how they're part of that picture. Either way, information about new initiatives needs to be 'revealed' in a way that entices people to know more and, ultimately, to participate.

Both marketers and managers can learn this from the striptease theory of marketing: simply producing information is not enough. You have to tantalise your target audience – whether they're employees or prospects – so that they *want* to engage with your message.

In order to make people want it more, marketers should do one of more of the following things.

- Peel back the layers of information one at a time, and carefully reveal each piece with a flourish.
- Give people what they desire (not just what you think they need).

- Romance the audience (make them excited about what they're getting).
- Dress up your content appropriately (graphics and layout make content a whole lot more appealing).
- And always leave them wanting more…

Similarly, simply giving people information about a new element of work is not enough. Employees – the vanguard of your Secret Army – want to feel like they're part of something, part of a group that gives them an identity and makes their work worthwhile. In order to help get and keep them engaged, managers can learn from burlesque artists too.

When revealing new initiatives, managers should do one or more of the following things.

- Help them peel back layers of meaning, one at a time, in their contributions to work and in their own career evolution.
- Give people what they desire *and* what they need at work.
- Romance them (make them excited about what they're doing).
- Keep the office environment appealing.

In the end, marketers, managers and salespeople have a lot more in common that unifies rather than divides them. If, collaboratively, they embrace the insight that everyone needs to be sold to, then employees, customers and prospects become more engaged. As a result, it's far easier to get people to do what they're being asked to do: to buy in to your business, and to buy your products.

MAKING PEOPLE BUY YOUR STUFF – BECAUSE THEY WANT TO

So, how can employees and customers make people buy your products – because *they want to*? We addressed this question right at the beginning of the book, but it's worth repeating.

The answer is: when great marketing is aligned with great leadership and shares a common vision of success, something almost magical happens: everyone in the Secret Army is lured in. In this way, marketing can give customers what they secretly want, but didn't even know they wanted. Marketers, salespeople and leaders become allies in providing their customers with a solution to their problems. When marketers get it right, they tap into the psyche of their customers.

LESSONS FROM GREAT ADVERTISEMENTS

The chances are that at least one or two adverts have stuck in your mind over time.

Personally, I'll never forget the British Airways advert with hundreds of people of all nations coming together in the wilderness to make a huge face that winked, and then turned into a globe of the world, while the moving strains of classical music played powerfully in the background.[94]

Admittedly, the powerful music certainly helped the advert's memorability, but it's possible to do this without music too.

The recent example from Oasis – with the strapline 'refreshing stuff' – is highly memorable, not to mention refreshing. It simply states: 'It's summer. You're thirsty. We've got sales targets'.[95] It captures the psyche of a population of cynical consumers who know advertising exists to make them buy more stuff, but who are sick of being lied to or artificially enticed.

Or perhaps there's a video advert that you watched over and over again? For me, it was the Bertrum Thumbcat advert for Cravendale milk.[96] It postulated the idea that, if cats had thumbs, they'd take over the world by becoming 'an organised army with one thing on their mind'. That one thing was to take all the milk away from humans.

The point here is that these adverts are memorable because they connect with people. Powerful adverts make you laugh or touch your heart, they get your brain working, or trigger another powerful emotion – perhaps the need to belong, or even anger (some powerful campaigns that oppose things like smoking or drugs, or dropping litter, tap into these kinds of emotions).

The lesson adverts like these can teach people in business is this: if you can capture people's emotions, they're pre-aligned with your goals and are therefore more likely to work towards the same desired outcome.

Marketers know this; so do persuasive leaders.

So how do you leverage these powerful tools of engagement to take your company's message beyond its internal borders? It's called marketing amplification, and it works hand-in-hand with social selling and employee advocacy.

MARKETING AMPLIFICATION IS EVERYONE'S JOB

Good marketers know that even the best piece of content in the world – whether an e-book, a video or even an advert – is useless if people don't see it, share it or talk about it. This is why a 'campaign' designed to amplify the reach of the message should be at the heart of every marketing initiative.

A marketing campaign is composed of the target audience, key messages, the goals or expected outcomes, all the tools available at a marketer's disposal, and the plan of when and how to use those tools.

Marketers may use one or a dozen tools to get the right message to the right audience – partly because people consume information in different ways, and partly because it takes a long time (anecdotally, seven instances) before anyone even recognises the brand, never mind wants to buy anything.

Marketers can use email, social media, the telephone, direct mail, advertising and many, many more tools to reach their audience (and these are increasing all the time). But they have to find the right combination of the tools available at their disposal to keep reaching someone, because they never know exactly when that person is going to be interested in buying what they have to sell.

John Wanamaker, a very successful United States merchant, religious leader, political figure, and considered by some to be a 'pioneer in marketing', is believed to have said this gem: 'Half the money I spend on advertising is wasted; the trouble is I don't know which half.'[97]

However, marketing has evolved significantly since the dawn of the digital era. It's no longer a guessing game.

In fact, since the majority of marketing is done online these days, it can be relatively easy (if you've got the right analysis tools and abilities) to tell if marketing *is* working and, more importantly, how much it costs and what its return on investment is.

Marketing is also more sophisticated than ever before. Marketers are much better at identifying the people who are likely to be interested in buying their product or service (their 'target market'). And they're better at dividing their target market up into personas and understanding what makes them tick.[aa]

So, marketers have learned these things over time:

- who they're talking to,
- what the people (personas) are likely to be interested in, what their pain points or problems are, and how their product/service will solve this problem,
- how they can reach these people (using the various tools available to marketers),
- how much it's going to cost to reach these people, and
- the likelihood of success.

What they need, though, is a way to spread their messages, because all the planning in the world won't help if the messages aren't going to the right people.

This is where the concept of marketing amplification comes in. Campaigns are one way of making sure a message is heard, again and again, but it isn't a way of getting messages to more and more people. That's where social media can help – and it's also the point when marketing stops being only the marketer's problem, and starts becoming the whole company's challenge to resolve.

Thanks to social media, it's now possible to share messages that were previously only available to a selected list, with a far broader audience.

[aa] For more information on personas see Chapter 3.

Social media works on these simple principles.

- People like connecting with people.
- If people like something, they'll share it.
- People trust people.
- If people have shared something with someone they trust, the 'sharee' is more likely to trust that information too (or, at least, more likely to pay attention to it and respond to it).

At first, social media was simply a tool for individuals to share information with their peer group, or boast about their latest exploits. Then social media evolved into the domain of business. Then social media got organised, thanks to groups, tags and hashtags. This enabled people who are interested in a specific topic to find what they're looking for more easily.

Social media works because people share information they find IRATE: Interesting, Relevant, Appropriate, Timely and Entertaining. Actually, IRATE content does exactly the opposite of make people irate: it makes them interested, keeps them interested, and helps them help themselves.

Enter the dawn of 'social selling'.

One of the early pioneers of this concept, Jill Rowley, used social selling as the bedrock of her sales strategy – a tactic that earned her numerous awards and made her Eloqua's top-performing salesperson year after year after year. She won the 2011 Eloquan of the Year, and the Stevie Awards' 2013 Sales Representative of the Year (to name a few – there are more awards on her LinkedIn profile if you want to check it out).[98]

They called her the 'Eloqueen'.

How did she do it? She connected with people.

Since leaving Eloqua, she has, in fact, turned the art of social selling into a lucrative business, and follows her own advice: she uses the principle of ABC, but turns it on its head. In the sales world, ABC used to mean 'always be closing'. For her, it stands for 'always be connecting'. She made sales by providing people with helpful, interesting information that led, indirectly, back to her brand. She provided advice on the problems her target audience needed to solve so that, when they couldn't solve it themselves, they came to her to help them – *et voilà*, she turned that into a sale. Today, she has more than 112,000 followers on LinkedIn – all of them eating up her helpful content.

SOCIAL SELLING FOR BUSINESSES

Now, we're not all going to be champion salespeople – but we don't need to be. The secret power of your Secret Army of employees and customers lies in their networks. The way to use this secret power is simple.

- Ask them.
- Earn the right.
- Keep earning the right.

This three-step process works for social selling, marketing, recruitment, brand awareness – indeed, for almost any message sharing that is genuinely helpful for people.

- Firstly, ask people if they'll share information on your behalf. A lot of happy and engaged employees are very willing to the share information their company produces if it reflects well on the company, is something IRATE or helpful, just amuses them, or touches an emotional nerve.
- That's a very big 'if', though – in order to earn the right to have your employees, customers, advocates and even followers share information, they have to *want to share* the information.
- And to keep them sharing that information, you have to keep earning the right to have them share your stuff: that means you have to keep treating them well, fairly, and with respect. Sharing good stuff will also continually keep them engaged.

It's a never-ending circle of psychology, and it's more important than ever before, because that virtuous sharing circle can go both ways. If employees, customers, advocates and followers become unhappy, they can just as quickly and easily share information that provides negative information about your company or initiatives (that's where internet trolls came from, and they're dangerous and demonic, like their name). Do not despair, however. Once they've had their say, dissatisfied social sharers will, more often than not, pipe down and let the hubbub fall away.

Indeed, it's even possible for unhappy customers to be turned around: if a bad experience is dealt with in a positive way and if the company or customer service representatives go *beyond* the call of duty, then a dissatisfied customer can even be turned into an advocate, someone who will go the extra mile in order to recommend the company. So even the bad parts of the internet and social sharing can have an upside.

In short, messages will get out there – more quickly than was even imaginable in the past – because people enjoy sharing information, and the internet (specifically, social media) has made it possible to share instantly.

If you ask your employees to share information, those who do so will share it for various reasons: perhaps to grow their own following, to look like an expert, because they want to amuse others, or just because they enjoy sharing things that touch their emotions. It's in your best interests as a leader to help them share your company's information by making it shareable – that is, not just 'possible to be shared', but evocative enough for people to *want* to share it.

Social media is one of the most powerful tools available to your marketing team and, ultimately, to your business. It also makes it far easier for your salespeople to sell – because, when social selling is done right, your prospective customers don't even feel like they're being 'sold to'.

In this way, the power of marketing – in combination with your Secret Army – can give your customers what they secretly want, but didn't even know they wanted.

> **LESSON 14:** Communication is an extremely powerful weapon in your arsenal. Making people *want* to share information helps them, and you.

Key Takeaways:

- *Both marketers and managers can learn this from the striptease theory of marketing: simply producing information is not enough. You have to tantalise your target audience – whether they're employees or prospects – so that they want to engage with your message.*

- *If you can capture people's emotions, then they'll be pre-aligned with your goals and are therefore more likely to work towards the same desired outcome.*

- *Social media works because people share information they find IRATE: Interesting, Relevant, Appropriate, Timely and Entertaining.*

- *It's in leaders' best interests to make information shareable – that is, not just 'possible to be shared', but evocative enough for people to want to share it.*

Chapter 16: Voice of the Customer

What do your customers really want? We give some insight into why it might not be what you think they want, and how to discover the difference between the two. We also reveal the importance of customer experience and its value across the whole customer lifecycle, as well as your brand. And we include two great examples that explain good and bad customer experience, as well as a model that could help us understand what satisfies your customers.

WHAT DO YOUR CUSTOMERS WANT?

If you've got a successful business and it's growing year on year and you're making a profit, you'll likely assume that you know what your customers want – because you're already giving it to them.

You're partly right: those indicators show that you do, indeed, know what your customers want *now*.

But customers are fickle these days.

You may have an extremely loyal brand following who will forgive the occasional product disaster and carry on loving what you do and buying every new version that you bring out (instances of this are extremely rare, but they do exist – Apple is one such example). But even if you do have an adoring, loyal customer base, you can only assume that you're pleasing them at the moment. Unfortunately, there's no guarantee you'll always be able to please them.

So how do you find out what your customers want before they know it themselves?

This is where research and development teams come in, and where a truly deep understanding of the customer experience is absolutely essential because, as we just covered, if customers are *not* happy with what you do, it doesn't just affect *them* anymore.

Once upon a time, when customers were unhappy, they would stop buying your product and that would be the end of it. Of course, they'd tell their friends and family and people at work, and there was a risk that the word would spread, but there was likely to be a limited reach to the impact of their dissatisfaction. Now, there's a whole world out there that's listening 24/7. Social media has made it possible to share great customer examples – but it's also possible to share whinges, rants and horror stories.

So, I ask again, what do your customers want? Do you know? And what are you doing to make sure that you're giving them what they want, consistently? Are you looking deeper, anticipating what they'll want in future and starting to work on producing that before your competitors do? You should be.

It's a tall order, but there are things you can do to help your customers and your business. The good news is that often this one activity serves a dual purpose.

CUSTOMER EXPERIENCE

A trend that has taken on epic proportions over the last few years is 'customer experience'. Here's how it's defined:

> In commerce, customer experience (CX) is the product of an interaction between an organization and a customer over the duration of their relationship.[99]

In simple terms, customer experience is the sum of the experience your customer has with your brand/company – *at any and all* points in time.

Those occasions when they interact with anyone from your company are called 'touchpoints'. A series of touchpoints across a customer's lifecycle all contribute towards their entire experience. This is why it's critical for businesses to understand their customers' or buyers' journey – from the first moment they're exposed to the brand (this may be via marketing, word of mouth or even as a job-seeker) until the end of their time with you.

How the buyers' journey applies to your role in a business depends on how you interact with customers during their buying process.

- If you're in marketing, you'll be concerned with their journey from first brand exposure to their hand-off to sales (or, more likely these days, until the sale closes).
- If you're in sales, you'll be focused on how to get them from a warm lead to a closed lead.
- If you're in implementation, or any other kind of process that's involved from the moment they make a decision to purchase something until that 'thing' has actually been delivered, then your part of the journey ends when they have received their finished goods or the service has been completed.[bb]
- If you're in the support function, your view of the buyers' journey is limited to what happens once they've purchased that product or service and start to complain about it.
- If you're in renewals, you'll know that their journey before they got to you is critical, but there's not much you can do about it until it's time to sweet-talk them into renewing their contract or re-purchasing their old/redundant/outdated item.

But if you're in the company's leadership team, you should be concerned about their interaction with your brand – and that includes all the people who are associated with your brand, whether they are directly employed by your company or not – *at all times*! Why? Because every single interaction your customers have with any one of them can make or break that relationship with your company, your brand or your product.

It takes many, many interactions to make a good impression – but only one to ruin that impression. Consequentially, it is vitally important that the people with whom your customers interact are happy with your product or service, and are likely to be promoters. Of course, you can't control every single person's attitude, but you can certainly do your best to find out what their attitudes are and ensure that they're as positive as possible.

[bb] The same applies if you're building a bespoke piece of furniture, or your customer is waiting for their new car.

This means that every single person in the chain: your marketers, salespeople, customer support people, customers and even your providers, is potentially part of your Secret Army!

This is why it's so important to make sure that as many of them as possible are happy – because they tell other people about their experiences, and because those experiences or brand 'touchpoints' can ruin an otherwise brilliant reputation if they're not happy.

AN EXAMPLE: INNOCENT SMOOTHIES

Here's an example: when Innocent first started making smoothies, they did a lot of brand outreach. They drove around in vans carpeted in artificial grass and handed out free smoothies. They did advertising that talked about their 'all-natural' approach with a humorous, open tone of voice; they even got volunteers to knit little woollen hats for their smoothies in winter, and donated the cost of making the hats to worthy causes.

Their tone was irreverent, engaging and fun. They even invited people to write to them at 'Fruit Towers' (their London office address), or call them on their 'bananaphone'.

I loved their smoothies, and I loved their brand.

I even started buying their veggie pots. I was a loyal customer and, in fact, a fan. I totally bought into their ethos – I felt good about buying food items made with good stuff inside by good people who were making good food.

And then I sent them an email. In it, I spoke about how much I loved their smoothies, but explained that I had recently noticed that they were making them less thick and more juicy/watery. I specifically wrote it in their jokey, friendly tone of voice, expecting a similarly engaging reply.

But I was sadly disappointed.

Basically, their response was 'if you don't like it, lump it'. Okay, it wasn't as blunt as that – it was polite, at least, but still very dismissive. The very least I thought they could have done was offer me a free smoothie (which probably costs them around 50p to produce, if that) or a voucher, or something! But, no, there was nothing.

A few months later, I realised they had been taken over by a global beverage conglomerate. And that's where my love affair with the brand ended.

I stopped being a brand advocate, and if there was a competitive brand on the shelves when I bought a smoothie, I'd choose that one instead. While I didn't 'take to Twitter' to complain about the lower banana content in their smoothies (there's more apple juice these days, which is why they're less thick: apples are cheaper), I certainly told everyone I could that they had been acquired by a multi-national conglomerate and that I wouldn't recommend them anymore. Their single instance of an email response put me off purchasing any of their products for life. You may argue that, as it's just a few pounds per smoothie, does it really matter if they've lost me as a customer? Yes, it does. Why? Lifetime value.

> Customer Lifetime Value describes the amount of revenue or profit a customer generates over his or her entire lifetime.[100]

The lifetime value of a loyal consumer, even for something as cheap as smoothies, is crazily high. That's why fast-moving consumer goods brands (otherwise known as consumer packaged goods) spend so much money on advertising.

If a brand is familiar, it becomes the default purchase – over years and years and years. Think about it: unless you've moved countries or something put you off the brand, you're probably still buying the same brand of cleaning material or toilet paper that you bought ten years ago.

I certainly know that one of the most annoying things, for me, about moving from the Southern Hemisphere to the Northern Hemisphere was having to build up a new understanding of brand values and choosing new 'lifetime' brands – for everything from toothpaste to spaghetti!

Familiar brands give customers comfort, and the profit a company will make back from customers because they don't want to expend the mental effort to choose a new brand each time they make a routine purchase is enormous.

Yes, the smoothie manufacturer *should* have cared that I stopped being a loyal fan and became what is known in marketing circles as a detractor (someone who will actively talk against the brand).

But when brand loyalty goes right, as it hopefully does with most of your customers most of the time, then it becomes a positive, collaborative experience that helps you win new customers – for free – because your existing customers love you and what you do.

WHY GIVING STUFF AWAY FOR FREE IS GOOD BUSINESS PRACTICE

There's actually a second part to my Innocent story. It starts with a mug.

A few months ago, Innocent advertised that they were giving away free coffee cups to customers who purchased large bottles of their smoothies. As it turned out, I was one of them. Over time, my dissatisfaction with the brand had lessened. I had forgiven what I perceived as their sell-out to a global beverage conglomerate, and started buying their smoothies again. So, when I saw this offer, I jumped at the chance to test their customer loyalty.

I was blown away by the experience.

My mug arrived, very safely wrapped up, with a lovely note from them. And it was a good mug. It reflected their old values and made me, as a customer, very happy. (Plus, it was free!) So I tweeted them. And something very nice happened. They replied to my tweet.

Then something even better happened – we started a conversation.

Gina Balarin
@GBalarin

Loving the gift from @innocent. Thanks guys! Great #customerexperience #cx #custexp 😊

9:58 AM - 23 Jan 2017

1 Like   SQ

💬 1   🔁   ♡ 1   ⬛

Tweet your reply

innocent drinks ✅ @innocent · Jan 23
Replying to @GBalarin
entirely our pleasure, Gina. Tea will have never tasted so good.

💬   🔁   ♥ 1   ✉

This series of tweets, over the course of a few days, transformed the way I felt about Innocent entirely. I am now a fan; a brand advocate. I even tell this story of a successful customer experience over Twitter when I speak at marketing events.

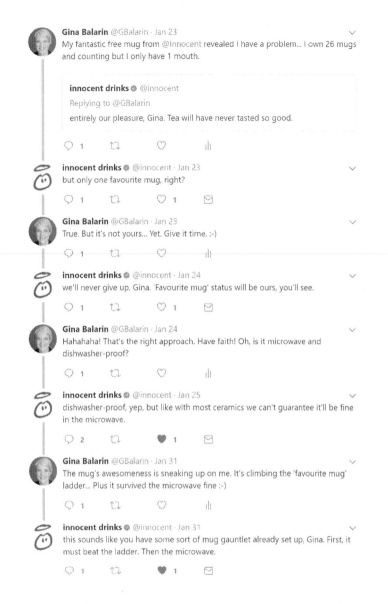

Gina Balarin @GBalarin · Jan 23
My fantastic free mug from @Innocent revealed I have a problem... I own 26 mugs and counting but I only have 1 mouth.

> **innocent drinks** ● @innocent
> Replying to @GBalarin
> entirely our pleasure, Gina. Tea will have never tasted so good.

○ 1   ⟲   ♡   �╎╎╎

innocent drinks ● @innocent · Jan 23
but only one favourite mug, right?

○ 1   ⟲   ♡ 1   ✉

Gina Balarin @GBalarin · Jan 23
True. But it's not yours... Yet. Give it time. :-)

○ 1   ⟲   ♡   ╎╎╎

innocent drinks ● @innocent · Jan 24
we'll never give up, Gina. 'Favourite mug' status will be ours, you'll see.

○ 1   ⟲   ♡ 1   ✉

Gina Balarin @GBalarin · Jan 24
Hahahaha! That's the right approach. Have faith! Oh, is it microwave and dishwasher-proof?

○ 1   ⟲   ♡   ╎╎╎

innocent drinks ● @innocent · Jan 25
dishwasher-proof, yep, but like with most ceramics we can't guarantee it'll be fine in the microwave.

○ 2   ⟲   ♥ 1   ✉

Gina Balarin @GBalarin · Jan 31
The mug's awesomeness is sneaking up on me. It's climbing the 'favourite mug' ladder... Plus it survived the microwave fine :-)

○ 1   ⟲   ♡   ╎╎╎

innocent drinks ● @innocent · Jan 31
this sounds like you have some sort of mug gauntlet already set up, Gina. First, it must beat the ladder. Then the microwave.

○ 1   ⟲   ♥ 1   ✉

The bottom line is that Innocent may not have immediately been able to demonstrate return on investment (for more on ROI, see Chapter 11) on its free giveaway of mugs, but it will more than make up for that in the increased life-time value they'll get out of me as a customer And because I'm willing – nay, delighted – to share the success story, this gift of a mug and the associated effort and sense of humour of their Twitter manager at the time will (I hope) go on to persuade many more customers that Innocent has learned to love its customers again and we, in turn, can love them back.

To conclude the Innocent story: it might look like I was 'bought' with a free mug, but it's not about the mug – or not *only* about the mug. It's about the fact that the brand found its way back to its original roots – a good brand that made good stuff and shared its passion with people in a quirky, engaging way. They re-discovered their voice and, as a result, were able to re-engage with customers who hadn't entirely stopped loving them, yet, or were willing to forgive them and try them again.

They're just one example of great brands doing great things over time that are worth celebrating.

These stories are particularly worth sharing because marketing is *hard* and marketers need to know when they're doing things right – particularly because the impact of good marketing can sometimes be felt long after the campaigns have ended.

Here's an example of brand loyalty that caused me to become a customer, and then a fan, and then a brand advocate, for a company that understood its audience so well that it won me over years before I first purchased their product.

The company is called HubSpot.

They're a marketing automation software leader and one of the early adopters, if not the originator, of the 'inbound' marketing movement. When I first came across them, many years ago, they were producing great marketing content that was helpful first, and sales-y second. (Actually, it was barely sales-y at all).

I met the person who was their Chief Marketing Officer at the time (Mike Volpe) at a marketing event and, to me, his approach epitomises the philosophy that underpins their ethos: help first, get people to buy second. He explained that their strategy was to give away content *for free* for the first 12 to 18 months of the company's outreach programme. I don't think they even collected people's email addresses initially. Then, a year and a half later (which is an aeon in most businesses), they started asking people for their contact details in order to get the valuable content. And the content *was* valuable. So valuable, in fact, that I bought in to their marketing philosophy.[cc]

It took nearly three years before I was in a position to choose marketing automation software – but when the time came, they were the forerunner for me.

I was delighted to finally become one of their customers, and told them so in a post I wrote on LinkedIn entitled 'Why HubSpot rocks – and its customers think so too'.[101] Something very cool happened once I sent that post – the HubSpot community of employees liked it. And they shared it. Even their founder and CTO, Dharmesh Shah, and their current CMO, Kipp Bodnar, put comments on my LinkedIn post. I was delighted, but that wasn't even the end of it! That post led to me getting an awesome account manager, Georgianne Papacostas, and to them asking me to do a video customer case study for them.[102] That eventually led to me speaking at more than one of their events and meeting their CEO, Brian Halligan, who I am a huge fan of.[dd]

Over time, my relationship with HubSpot has evolved from me being a dewy-eyed wannabe purchaser to a worldly-wise product owner. Okay, their customer experience has had its ups and downs over time, but their customer support has also gone far beyond its boundaries (and my expectations). When I was made redundant, that very same account

---

[cc] I also, literally, bought the t-shirt – thanks to a voucher given to me by Mike Volpe. I still proudly wear it and delight in the words emblazoned across my chest 'My content brings all the leads to the yard'. It certainly has, in the past.

[dd] The highlight of my interactions with Brian has been when he replied to a LinkedIn message I sent him, with the words 'I'm a fan of yours.' It made my year, and has kept me loyal to HubSpot long since I've been able to use their product on a daily basis.

manager even helped me find a new job with another HubSpot customer. To me, this just goes to show that HubSpot is still being true to their ethos of being a helpful, valuable brand many, many years after I first bought into their vision as a prospective customer.

Why am I still a fan?

When I buy an Innocent smoothie, I expect to receive a healthy beverage that quenches my thirst and tastes good. Is that my minimum expectation, though? No. Because of the way they've positioned their brand in the market, I have higher expectations – I expect to be 'nourished' by their drink, to 'feel better or healthier' as a result of drinking it. I also expect their whole brand team to be on the same wavelength with their quirky, human and engaging approach. I was not satisfied until they turned around their customer experience and met my expectations.

However, when it came to HubSpot, I expected to receive good quality service, responsive replies to my queries, helpful advice and friendly support. And I got it. But what made me a 'delighter' is the fact that they went beyond my expectations. I didn't expect their CMO to comment on my blog post that featured him – but he did (it was a lovely, engaging and honest reply too). I didn't expect their CEO to accept my invitation to connect on LinkedIn, and I particularly did not expect him to say that he's a fan of mine, as much as I'm a fan of his, after I spoke at the same HubSpot event as him – but he did. I didn't expect my account manager to help me find a new job – but she did. To go back to the model that we covered almost at the beginning of this book, in the chapter about 'your customers' (i.e. the ladder of loyalty), I am proud to be a firm advocate of HubSpot. And that advocacy has happened as a direct result of them consistently exceeding expectations.

Keeping an eye on customer satisfaction is key to unlocking the value your customers get out of your brand. It's key to finding out what makes your customers happy, and keeping them happy, and it's worth tracking at every stage of the customer process. Indeed, whole books have been written about the subject of customer experience, huge conferences exist to talk about it, entire businesses are devoted to measuring it and making recommendations about how to identify and remedy weaknesses across the chain. It's an interesting subject that is worth pursuing more thoroughly, and is beyond the scope of this book.

CUSTOMER AND EMPLOYEE SATISFACTION

But there is one very important and highly relevant thought that's relevant for our Secret Army: if companies are doing this for their customers, why aren't they doing it for their employees?

The secret power of both your employees and your customers lies in their ability and their willingness to be brand advocates for your company; to willingly discuss what is great about your business because *they want to*. That, more than anything, is a secret weapon of business success.

> **LESSON 15:** Both your customers and your employees can be a secret weapon. Give them more than they expect, and the opportunity to share their delight. The result could be extraordinary success.

Key Takeaways:

- *If you're selling enough to know what your customers want now, are you looking deeper, anticipating what they'll want in future and starting to work on producing that before your competitors do? You should be.*

- *Once upon a time, when customers were unhappy they would stop buying your product and that would be the end of it. Now, there's a whole world out there with whom they can share stories of their dissatisfaction.*

- *If you're in the company's leadership team, you should be concerned about your customers' interaction with your brand at all times! Why? Because every single interaction your customers have can make or break that relationship with your company, your brand, or your product.*

- *Familiar brands give customers comfort, and the profit a company will make back from customers (their 'customer lifetime value') because they don't want to expend the mental effort to choose a new brand each time they make a routine purchase is enormous.*

- *A secret weapon available to your Secret Army lies with your employees and your customers. If they're able and willing to be brand advocates for your company, they will share what is great about your business because* they want to.

Chapter 17: Relationship Counselling for Sales and Marketing

Selling is human, so why do salespeople have such a bad reputation? We answer this question and talk about how sales and marketing are merging. We also cover the role of trust, and why it's important for sales and marketing to build ever stronger relationships with each other. The chapter ends with ten pieces of relationship-counselling advice for sales and marketing.

Daniel Pink, the author of *To Sell is Human*,[103] argues, convincingly, that everyone *can* sell – indeed, everyone *does* sell.

If you've ever tried to convince someone to babysit your kids or go to a movie with you, to give you a raise or persuade them to do something you want to do but they don't, then you've been a salesperson. Somehow, being a salesperson has pejorative connotations, as does being a marketer.

HubSpot did a study in 2016 on the 'trustworthiness' of various professionals, asking the question 'Who do you consider to be trustworthy?' to 928 people. When the results came in, marketers scored a three per cent level of trustworthiness. The only people who did worse than them were stockbrokers (two per cent) and car salesmen, politicians and lobbyists – who rated one per cent. Even coffee baristas got a higher ranking, achieving a five per cent trustworthiness rating.[104]

SO WHY DO SALESPEOPLE HAVE SUCH A BAD REP?

We may resent salespeople for trying to sell us items we don't want or need. Alternatively, it may be that salespeople have, in the past, been known to 'fudge the truth'. Think 'used-car salesman' – their job is to make the car so desirable that we'll overlook its obvious failings.

Once upon a time, specialised knowledge was stored in information siloes and the salesperson really *did* have all the information about the second-hand car available to him or herself. Buyers didn't have the power, the salesman did.

Today, however, the once ignorant buyer is firmly in control. Mostly thanks to the internet, it's no longer possible to bamboozle people, because information is now available on an unprecedented scale. Many, many websites exist that help people to check the registration and find out the car's entire history, or estimate its value in pounds, dollars or euros, before even taking it for a test-drive.

I like to believe that this era of authenticity is changing the world for the better. I like to think that it's giving people power and choice. However, while that is undoubtedly true, knowledge, and the availability of knowledge, is a double-edged sword. Yes, the information is available, but it's not always immediately obvious what information to believe. Like Dana Scully said in the X-Files, 'the truth is out there'. In other words, information is out there, but it's subjective, and it's often difficult to know who to trust. That's partly why sales and marketing need to team up with unlikely partners... their customers.

TWO SIDES OF THE SAME COIN[105]

Great salespeople know that in order to make someone buy something from you, you have to help them know they want it – and you have to get them to realise your truth: the truth that their lives will be better if they buy what you have to sell.

Only, in this day and age, salespeople and marketers seem to be doing more and more of each other's jobs. Salespeople are marketing. Marketers are selling.

Indeed, I think we're heading towards a world where sales and marketing are, in fact, merging. Soon, neither of us will be salespeople or marketers: we'll be 'sales-eters' or 'market-people'. But this is only possible if there's true collaboration between salespeople and marketers.

This increasingly close alignment of business units is certainly becoming more of a reality for marketing and sales than it has been in the past. It's not just about having the two departments under a single leader, a 'Head of Sales and Marketing', because, indeed, the two groups have entirely separate skills. No, it's more about aligning core objectives, making the two groups realise that together they are more than the sum of their parts, erasing misunderstandings and creating a shared view of success.

That's the leaders' job. But it's also the responsibility of every single salesperson, and every single marketer, to work together – for the benefits of their customers.

PROSPECTS TRUST EXISTING CUSTOMERS

Who do you trust? Clearly not salespeople or marketers – as the statistics suggest. No, you're more likely to trust people you know, people who have had the same or similar experiences to yours, people who express themselves credibly or who tell a good story. You're also more likely to trust people who tell the truth – and that means sharing the good, the bad, and the ugly information, not just the pretty bits.

There's a backlash against dishonesty that's taking place. Our era of authenticity demands full disclosure. Your employees expect it, and so do your customers.

As a result, what works brilliantly is when your employees *and* your customers *and* your sales and marketing teams *and* your management teams work together in that spirit of full disclosure.

It's harder than it seems, though – mostly because salespeople and marketers haven't always seen eye to eye.

Marketing's job is to woo and to attract potential contacts and, increasingly, to help contacts decide that they want to purchase a specific product or service. Sales' job is to close the deal. If we think back to our Marketing Striptease theory, explained in Chapter 15, marketers need to 'leave them wanting more', but sales needs to satisfy their desire for closure. It's an uneasy relationship at the best of times, and sometimes, like on occasion in many partnerships, they could do with a bit of counselling because, in many companies, if sales and marketing were in a relationship, they wouldn't be together for long!

RELATIONSHIP COUNSELLING FOR SALES AND MARKETING[106]

Any relationship can be hard work, no matter how much you like/love/respect each other. But in the sales/marketing relationship, you're usually starting with a pretty shaky foundation in the first place. Often marketers don't have a high opinion of salespeople. And salespeople feel similarly about marketers. The truth is, we don't always understand each other, know about each other's needs, or (honestly) really have much interest in making each other happy.

As salespeople and marketers, we can sometimes feel like we're in an arranged marriage, and our matchmakers haven't done their homework well. We have to collaborate to get what we need to do done, but beyond that we are often guilty of being a bit self-absorbed. We don't see how, by forging a stronger relationship, both of us could benefit.

This misalignment and misunderstanding often comes down to wanting different things from the relationship.

Let's assume that marketers' aims are to nurture someone who has never heard about a company/product/service before, to a stage where they can be, gently and safely, led to the arms of a salesperson. And the salesperson's aim? To close business, as simple as that, and to move a prospective customer from undecided to purchased. They should be complementary roles – two partners in the same marriage. But often, they aren't. It's a war: dangerous and ugly.

There are two casualties in the S&M war.

The first casualty is the customer. If they're getting different messages before and after they talk to a salesperson, there's a risk that they'll simply turn off and look elsewhere. The second casualty is the business. Here's a simple formula to explain it.

THE CONSEQUENCE OF SALES AND MARKETING WAR

P+C = NP
[Prospects + Confusion = No Purchase]

Fortunately, any two partners who really want to work together for the benefit of the children (customers) can heal the rift: if they want to, and if they're prepared to try hard enough. Although there are no quick-fixes when building or repairing any relationship, there are some things that can kick-start the process.

TIPS TO IMPROVE S&M RELATIONSHIPS

Listen to each other.

Find out what the other party's real needs are, don't just assume you know. Assumptions are inaccurate at best, dangerous at worst. Share your own genuine needs, honestly. Misunderstandings can be remedied by communicating openly, demonstrating a willingness to listen and understand.

Understand what drives your partner.

We are all motivated by different things. Find out what motivates your counterpart in sales or marketing. You may not always be able to give it to them, but at least you'll know what definitely won't work.

Speak the same language.

What does marketing mean when they say, 'We've brought in one hundred leads!' The salesperson may assume it means these leads are all ready to buy. The chances are that this isn't exactly what marketing meant (which is why leads are now often divided into Marketing Qualified Leads (MQLs) and Sales Qualified Leads (SQLs)). Only when sales and marketing are speaking the same language can they agree on realistic expectations and work together, and separately, to achieve these.

Share the love.

If you've had a huge success (i.e. new business wins), don't keep that joy to yourselves – share it with your partner. Make them feel part of the excitement. Because without their efforts, you wouldn't have got there in the first place.

Go on date nights.

Some of the best team-building events I've experienced have taken place when both sales and marketing teams have really let their hair down, opened up and had a good time together. Sharing each other's worlds means enjoying the success together, but taking the time to listen to their gripes too. Often an alcohol-lubricated chat makes for increased honesty, but it's also a great chance to build relationships and have fun together. Alcohol is not always required, of course, but sometimes it helps.

Keep the children happy.

Customers may not know that Mom & Dad (Sales & Marketing) are fighting, but if their 'parents' are working together rather than separately, they have much more energy to focus on the kids – rather than focusing on their own arguments. An aligned S&M force builds stronger, better customer relationships.

Get creative together, for the benefit of the children.

How else can you help your customers? Simple: ask them what they want. Marketers – don't forget that sales have strong relationships with customers. Use those relationships to get the information you need to assist other customers like them.

Build a strong house together.

Get your marketing materials right. Marketing often assumes that they know what prospects want, but salespeople spend more time with prospects than almost anyone else. While salespeople won't know how to execute the best marketing materials, they have a pretty good idea about what will work (and what won't). Getting a senior salesperson's perspective on marketing materials *before the campaign is sent out* is invaluable – if for no other reason than because there's no point in creating stuff salespeople won't use or share willingly.

Plan together for the future.

Know what your business wants to achieve and brainstorm about how you can make that happen, together, as equals. It's like saving for a house, or a Caribbean holiday as a family – if you set goals together, you'll work together more effectively to achieve them.

Keep talking.

Finally, make sure that you keep communicating once you've built a solid bridge between the two of you. Keep talking about success and how to support future successes, keep aligning goals, keep targeting the right customers and building behind-the-scenes support – or you might run the risk of getting back on the track towards divorce...

> **LESSON 16:** There's power in the Secret Army: the power to sell. We're all salespeople, fighting in some way to convince people to buy what we have to sell. But if we work together, our chances of success increase significantly.

Key Takeaways:

- *This simple formula explains why sales and marketing have to work together. It explains the consequence of a war between sales and marketing.*

    P+C = NP [Prospects + Confusion = No Purchase]

- *There are two casualties in the S&M war. The first casualty is the customer. The second casualty is the business.*

- *An aligned S&M force builds stronger, better customer relationships.*

- *Any two partners who really want to work together for the benefit of the children (customers) can heal the rift: if they want to, and if they're prepared to try hard enough.*

Chapter 18: People Buy from People

Why is it important to like the person who's selling something to you? And how can they use stories to convince you? We explain the 'golden moment' in customer storytelling, and provide ten tips to help you collect customer stories during that time.

To delve into the world of sales and marketing is to touch on fundamental human processes, including why we make the decisions we do. In a world where money gives us so many options, what makes people decide they want to exchange the money they could potentially spend on *anything* in order to buy *that particular thing*?

No-one (not even the person making the choice) can be entirely certain what helped them reach the final decision, no matter how they try to explain it, because people make decisions in complex, intricate, illogical and strangely irrational ways.[107] Indeed, most complex decisions are made emotionally and then justified rationally.

The fact that people themselves are complex, contrary and often strangely ignorant of their own reasons for doing things has important implications for anyone who wants to encourage them to do more of one thing and less of another. This includes sales, marketing, management and leadership.

As we discovered in Chapter 16, even when it comes to the simplest of apparent decisions (which grocery product to buy, such as toilet paper or beverages), a huge number of hidden factors are at play of which we are almost entirely unaware.

THE PSYCHOLOGY OF DECISION-MAKING

To understand the psychology of decision-making, it's worth taking a brief look at the ideas behind Malcolm Gladwell's book, *Blink. The power of thinking without thinking.*[108] It provides an articulate and easy-to-read explanation of how our brains make decisions – which is both more complicated and far simpler than you think.

In short, we have two separate systems of decision-making, one that processes routine information (such as buying toilet paper) and one that helps us make more complicated choices (like buying a car or deciding which school to send our children to).

But unbeknownst to us, these systems can work in harmony or in opposition. Our brain makes decisions we don't know about, and so the routine activities we end up doing become habit because we forget that we ever made a conscious choice to do them.

Similarly, we are guided by unconscious connections in our brains that inhibit us from making truly rational (i.e. completely non-emotional) decisions. This is why being a salesperson is both an art and a science, and why effective salespeople often have a deep understanding of human behaviour and psychology.

Some people have made it their jobs to understand why people make the decisions that they do.

- The best salespeople work hard to understand how to help people activate the triggers that will make them more likely to buy, and enormous volumes of literature have been written about how to make people buy more.
- Similarly, the best marketers help people identify what is great about the product or service their company provides in such a way that it helps potential customers decide to make that purchase.

At the end of the day, it is the marketers' job to expose their company's products or services to prospective customers in a way that will help them make the decision to purchase, and it's the salespeople's jobs to help convince their prospective customers to make that purchase. But people buy from people.

THE RIGHT SALESPEOPLE

Have you ever worked with a salesperson who didn't like their customers? I have. Things didn't go well.

This salesperson thought that her customers were ignorant, annoying and, above all, stupid. I will never forget hearing her speak to a customer on the phone in such a way that I was incredibly glad it wasn't me on the receiving end of the call. Suffice to say, the deal didn't close, despite her best efforts to apologise and rectify the situation later.

As we've covered throughout this book, today's salesperson has to do far more to understand his or her customer than they ever had to before. But, arguably, great salespeople have always done this. They know their customers, and they like them.

There's a reason I keep using the same estate agent.

I haven't bought or sold many houses in my lifetime. But when the time came to choose an estate agent to sell the property I had bought a few years ago, one name immediately sprang to mind: Warmingham & Co. They're a family-run estate agent that has one key differentiator: they care.

At first, when I was trying to sell my property, I made a big mistake. I engaged an estate agent who I didn't really like, and with whom I didn't have a shared experience, but who made big promises about how much they thought they could sell it for. Months later, I discovered they'd never had any intention of selling my property. No, they were using it as 'bait'. They had deliberately over-priced my flat so that they could point to other properties on their books as a much better deal and sell those instead. Suffice to say I was livid, and to this day I will denigrate that estate agent whenever I get the opportunity (I won't put their name in print, but if you want to know who not to buy from, drop me an email and if it's relevant, I'll tell you).

In contrast, Warmingham & Co (affectionately known as Warminghams) was there to pick up the pieces when I needed them. And they sold the property in record time. I believe their success comes down to these three factors: they like people, they like property and they're trustworthy.

While not every purchasing decision is as momentous as buying a house, we all tend to buy from people we like – and those we trust. The implication of this is that successful businesses should be careful to employ likeable, trustworthy salespeople – in addition to those who simply deliver results –

and make sure that their customers can hear the stories of others like them, warts and all, to gain or build that trust.

This means that it is someone's job to collect those stories, collate them and store them for future reference. Usually this is the job of the marketing department or, often, a marketer responsible for 'customer marketing'. But marketers aren't nearly as close to customers as the customer service or the sales teams are. This means that it's often very hard for marketing teams to know when the right time is to reach out to customers.

This makes life very hard for those responsible for story-gathering. I've worked with marketers who were terrified of asking for case studies because they never wanted to accidentally call an unhappy client. I've also worked with over-protective salespeople who never wanted their customers to be called by marketing in case marketing did something to jeopardise a potential deal.

So what is the answer? Regular, honest and sometimes painful communication between every stakeholder involved in the customer relationship, so that when the time comes to pick great stories from happy customers, it's easy to find those customers and, therefore, easy to collect the stories. I call these optimal collection times the 'golden moment'.

In every relationship, there are moments of pure gold when both participants are delighted with the way things are going. When it comes to business relationships, that's the time to catch the best recommendation from your customer, so that you can use (and re-use) it in your marketing activities.

WHEN IS THE 'GOLDEN MOMENT' FOR YOUR CUSTOMER?[109] WHEN...

- Your salespeople have sold exactly what your customers expected to receive (neither undersold nor oversold).
- The customer on-boarding experience went well.
- The product is doing what they expected it to do.
- The customer's customers (in software terms, their end-users) are happy.
- In short, the customer is delighted with your product(s) or service(s).

This is the time when your marketing team can swoop in and sweep up a glorious testimonial that shows the true value of your product/service. Because, at this moment in time, your customer isn't just happy; they are an advocate.

But capturing that golden moment is only half of the story. What comes before, and what happens next, is the secret to capturing that golden moment (that point when your customer loves you) and making it last forever.

It can be done by anyone with a true passion for collecting stories, but there is a specific talent to encouraging people to part with their stories. The tips below will help you do it – and it is possible. Collecting more than nineteen customer case studies in one year (my personal best, so far) took a lot of hard work, and I got my fair share of unanswered calls. But thanks to collaboration between sales teams, marketing teams, customers and account managers, as well as a focused approach and a genuine interest in people, we got it done. I also created and managed spreadsheets, called *lots* of customers, asked nicely, and made sure that any negative feedback was passed back to the appropriate people in the organisation so that they could get any unhappy customers back on-side again.

TEN TIPS THAT WILL HELP YOU CAPTURE THE GOLDEN MOMENT

1. Build relationships across the business so that your customer has a strong experience throughout their time with you.
2. Get someone they know and trust to introduce your interviewer.
3. Always be polite, friendly and helpful.
4. Set expectations up front – let them know what the process will be and what's expected of them.
5. Smile on the phone when you speak with them, especially during the interview process.
6. Type-up or record the interview as it's taking place – so you capture their real words, not a summary of them.

7. Write and deliver the case study when you say you will.
8. Always make sure they can add to or amend the case study before it's live.
9. Make it pretty (clean, clear design; no spelling or grammatical errors; strong callouts and enough white space).
10. Be honest.

And, of course, make sure that your customer is kept happy throughout the process. Because a golden moment may just be one point in time, but it requires a lot of effort to keep the customer happy enough for them to go up the ladder of loyalty, from being a customer, to being a supporter, to being an advocate for your product/service.

In summary: while your employees are the front-line of your business and selling your product or service is the victory you hope to achieve, it's simply not possible without your customers and your marketing team's ability to share those stories with the world. These stories are an essential weapon in your arsenal.

> **Lesson 17:** People buy from people. Your prospects want to trust you, so make it easy for them. Collect your customers' stories at the golden moment when they're newly delighted: these stories can be one of the most powerful weapons in your arsenal.

Key Takeaways:

- *The art and science of effective selling that drives effective business-building often derives from a deep understanding of the idiosyncrasies of human behaviour.*

- *We buy from people we like and trust. Companies need to make sure that their customers can hear the stories of others like them, warts and all, because it makes the company more trustworthy.*

- *In every relationship, there are moments of pure gold when both participants are delighted with the way things are going. That's the time to catch the best recommendation from your customer.*

Summary

The Secret Army has woven marketing experiences, leadership lessons, business models and human stories into a single narrative. It has looked at the difference people can make when they're inspired to do great things, and reflected on three groups of people: employees, customers and leaders.

By going back to the basics of what people really need to come alive, and why it's important to understand and care about *why* you do what you do, it has built a new way of thinking about these three groups of people – employees, customers and leaders – and highlighted the power they have to make a difference when they collaborate.

In Section One, we talked about how treating employees, customers and leaders as human beings can help them be more highly motivated which, in turn, improves productivity. We considered why having autonomy, mastery and purpose in a job also gives people an increased sense of meaning in their own lives, and helps our perpetual search for happiness.

We looked at the role customers – the first division in the Secret Army – play in the success of businesses. We discussed why it's important to truly understand your customers (although sleeping with them perhaps goes a bit far) and why people buy things. To aid this, we introduced the concept of creating personas as a way of categorising customers – and used the evolution of marketing and the theory of the ladder of loyalty to help identify customer stories that can increase sales and improve profits.

The next division of the Secret Army is the management team. We covered the differences between true leadership and mere management through the story of an influential leader who broke people's hearts when he left a business – but also inspired them to become leaders in their own right. We learned some lessons from Sun Tzu, and talked about the surprisingly different traits of Level 5 Leaders, who take companies from good to great.

And then we looked inward at the process of finding happiness, and in doing so, at the third division in the

Secret Army: the employees. We investigated the things that make us 'itchy' and how to capture people's hearts and minds. With a brief re-visit to the concepts of autonomy, mastery and purpose, we concluded that management's power lies in choosing the right people who fit in with the company. The other cohort of the Secret Army, the employees, has power too – but also the obligation to make happiness their own responsibility, particularly when they can move forward in a single direction because they are inspired to do it and can see themselves as part of a bigger picture.

In Section Two, we answered the question 'Who *are* you, anyway?' using the concepts of simplification and amplification, and took a look at the useful tactic of asking 'why' five times to get to the real reason behind doing anything, and pondered the definition of success. Then we turned our thoughts to the need for a company to have a clear vision, and discussed the problem with strategy as a concept. To assist us, we considered the differences between good and bad strategies.

Section Three was about the truth-tellers, guerrilla leaders, idea-generators and frustrated storytellers in organisations. These are the people who can identify what's really going on behind the scenes, who know how to inspire the Secret Army – for good or ill – and who have the creativity and the stories that can be used to inspire change.

In Section Four, we started searching for the hidden leaders within the organisation – those who can make or break change because of their ability to influence leaders in the company, and then looked at the art of making change possible in order to unlock 'yes'. This saw us examine the story of a pre-competitor, and draw inspiration in the form of lessons for intra-company connection and collaboration.

Section Five investigated the critical roles marketers, salespeople and customers play in our current digital era. Referring to the striptease theory of content marketing, we concluded with a revisit of the idea behind why people buy from people.

Our journey has gone from realising who the Secret Army really is, what role they can play in an organisation and how they can be encouraged or led to inspire change, to actually using marketing tactics in order to help companies sell more of their product or service.

In conclusion: these are the lessons for leadership from each chapter.

LEADERSHIP LESSONS FROM *THE SECRET ARMY*

Lesson 1: your employees are the largest regiment in your Secret Army. Most of them *want* to do a good job. Treating them like human beings is good for them, and good for business.

Lesson 2: your customers are a critical part of your Secret Army – but they can work *for* or *against* you. They need proof to be convinced to stay on your side.

Lesson 3: your Secret Army can be supported or destroyed by your generals (managers and leaders).

Lesson 4: your generals need to have people's hearts in mind.

Lesson 5: knowing why we do what we do makes fighting a war *worth fighting*. To keep your Secret Army fighting for your side, people need to understand what work means, and why it matters.

Lesson 6: every army needs a strategy to win the war. Get strategic in a meaningful way by building a vision that is easy to execute and figuring out how to do it. Then delete the 'fluff' that distracts people.

Lesson 7: your truth-tellers are a source of surprising insight and potential strategy that can power or inspire your Secret Army. Listen to them.

Lesson 8: sometimes the trouble-makers in your army are just leaders looking for a place to lead. Don't simply discipline them or, worse, kick them out. Give them more responsibility.

Lesson 9: the power of people in your Secret Army lies in the stories they tell. Stories make meaning of experiences and bring clarity and context. Empower your people; tell more stories.

Lesson 10: ideas are the building-blocks of greatness. They can come from any regiment of your Secret Army – but specifically from those on the front lines. Make time for them, listen for ideas from unexpected sources and build them into business as usual.

Lesson 11: hidden influencers determine your army's strategy, and can even be more powerful than leaders. They are the 'neck' that turns the leaders' heads. Get them on board, and your team will thrive.

Lesson 12: your Secret Army wants to do better if they can understand why it's worth doing. Help them get there – plan for change, lead it, and use your cheerleaders to help you.

Lesson 13: don't let an 'us/them' mentality invade your Secret Army. Breaking down barriers helps us be more human. Collaborating with others helps to build success.

Lesson 14: communication is an extremely powerful weapon in your arsenal. Making people *want* to share information helps them, and you.

Lesson 15: both your customers and your employees can be a secret weapon. Give them more than they expect, and the opportunity to share their delight. The result could be extraordinary success.

Lesson 16: there's power in the Secret Army: the power to sell. We're all salespeople, fighting in some way to convince people to buy what we have to sell. But if we work together, our chances of success increase significantly.

Lesson 17: people buy from people. Your prospects want to trust you, so make it easy for them. Collect our customers' stories at the golden moment when they're newly delighted: these stories can be one of the most powerful weapons in your arsenal.

I hope that this book has been thought-provoking and helpful, and look forward to hearing your responses. You can contact me, via Twitter (@GBalarin) or on LinkedIn (search for Gina Balarin and please indicate you've read this book when you invite me to connect with you), or email **comments@the-secret-army-book.com** to give me your comments and feedback.

If you have any thoughts on what The Secret Army should cover next, or want to share any of your own stories of success or failure, along with lessons learned, please get in touch!

Acknowledgements

If you're reading this page, congratulations! It means one of three things: you're very thorough, you've contributed meaningfully towards this book, or you're looking for insights about my publisher or agent. If one, I hope you've found it interesting. If two, I hope I haven't forgotten you – if I have, please contact me and I'll do my best to apologise in person. If three, sorry – no insights. I am my own agent, and Amazon CreateSpace is my route to market.

Seriously, though, there are lots of people to thank. In no particular order, here they are.

Firstly, I'd like to thank my parents, who are both natural-born storytellers and businesspeople. I've learned so much from you guys, even when I didn't realise I was learning it.

Thanks to all my employers. There have been many of them over the years and we've all got something out of working together, even if it was just learning about what not to do. However, I've also been incredibly fortunate to have had some amazing bosses and met some amazing leaders, including, but not limited to, these fine folks listed in alphabetical order below:

- Anita Marsh
- Bob Godfrey
- Francis Mdlongwa
- Henry Stewart
- Louisa Clayton
- Mike Hilton
- Patrick Drake
- Peter Clayton
- Peter Du Toit
- Raj Singh
- Steve Singh

There are also people who have been inspirational in the production of this book and whose stories I've used (with permission, wherever possible). Although the stories may not be recognisable to anyone but yourself and me, you've made a huge impact on my life and my perception of leadership, marketing and the power of people, and I'm very grateful. In alphabetical order, they are:

- Brian Halligan
- Glynn Coupland
- Govin Reddy
- Jenny Thornton
- Jill Rowley
- John Gooch
- Melissa Romo
- Mike Volpe
- Nick Whiteley
- Raphael Gouveia
- Ron Finley
- Simone Vincenzi
- Steve Kemish

There are many great authors quoted in here, but without the wise words of these truly inspiring ones, this book would simply not have been possible. Thank you for leading the way: Malcolm Gladwell, Mihaly Csikszentmihalyi, Henry Stewart, Charles Duhigg, Matthew D. Lieberman, Dan Ariely, Greg McKeown, and Daniel H. Pink.

Other highly influential (and readable) authors referenced here include David Taylor, Jeffrey J. Fox, Jonah Berger, Jim Collins, Jeff Hadden, Philip Kotler, Ricardo Semler, Richard Rumelt, Max McKeown, Chip and Dan Heath, Richard Templar and John Wanamaker.

Some brand stories have been particularly meaningful to me in the writing of this book. They include, but are not limited to:

- BrightTALK
- Concur
- HubSpot
- Innocent
- Passle

- Spiceworks
- Warmingham & Co Property Consultancy

Trustworthy sources make or break the credibility of a piece of work. Without these incredibly helpful organisations and their willingness to share knowledge for the benefit of others, I would have been lost. Thank you Healthline, Anxiety UK and CALM (and your very cool and clever Man dictionary).

Thanks go to the people who have published the blog posts I've written about marketing over the years. I'm so grateful to Cyance and Penquin, amongst others, for publishing those posts – I bet you never thought you were enabling a future book to emerge from this! LinkedIn has also been incredibly important in the production of this book. If I hadn't starting writing and publishing my own posts on their platform years ago, this book would never have been possible.

Similarly, I'm also incredibly grateful to those people who have enabled me to share stories in a digital format that then made their way into print. To Joel Harrison of B2BMarketing, whose team has had me on stage more than once; Mark Binns, for organising TEDx Reading 2016; and Beverley Sunderland, who kept bringing me back for enjoyable chats with TalkOxfordshire TV – thank you for helping me realise my dream to tell stories in public.

My beta readers were Jonathan Kittow, James Wilkinson, Jamie Nichols, Bronwen Eckstein and Donovan Shell. You guys took something that was okay and helped me get it to a place where I was proud (and unafraid) to publish it. Thank you!

To the people who helped kick off the social media sharing that helped me to crowd-verify the book cover (you know who you are!), thank you. And to the 2,266 (and counting) people who liked or commented on that single LinkedIn post, every single one of you has helped make something amazing happen. You rock!

To my awesome husband, who helped make this book a reality – even if you didn't believe it would ever see the light of day – I'm so grateful for the way you did (and didn't) push me to get it done and for all the bits of help (large and small) you've given me through the process and give me every single day. I love you.

And last, but probably most importantly, to my patient, talented, dedicated and tenacious editor, Laurel C Kriegler. I knew writing a book would be hard, but without your involvement I never would have got through the editing process that is so much harder (and more time-consuming) than I ever could have imagined. You are a marvel and I'm so grateful to you!

Endnotes

CHAPTER 1: WE ARE NOT ALONE

[1]   Matthew D. Lieberman. 2013. *Social: Why Our Brains Are Wired to Connect*, New York: Broadway Books, Random House.

[2]   HSE. 2016. *Work related stress, anxiety and depression statistics in Great Britain, 2016*. Retrieved 09 January 2017 from http://www.hse.gov.uk/statistics/causdis/stress/

[3]   MailOnline. 2013. *The stress factor that's costing the UK £10billion a year: Eight million Britons suffer from an anxiety disorder*. Retrieved 09 January 2017 from http://www.dailymail.co.uk/news/article-2377254/Stress-costing-UK-10billion-year-Eight-million-Britons-suffer-anxiety-disorder.html

[4]   Anxiety UK. 2016. Facts and Stats. A collection of up to date statistics on anxiety and mental health. Reviewed October 2016

[5]   WHO. 2017. *Depression*. Retrieved 03 April from http://www.who.int/mediacentre/factsheets/fs369/en

[6]   Healthline. 2012. *Depression Statistics: Unhappiness by Numbers [INFOGRAPHIC]*. Retrieved 15 December 2016 from http://www.healthline.com/health/depression/statistics-infographic

[7]   Anxiety UK. *Frequently Asked Questions*. Retrieved 15 December 2016 from https://www.anxietyuk.org.uk/our-services/anxiety-information/frequently-asked-questions/

[8]   McManus, S., Bebbington, P., Jenkins, R., Brugha, T. (eds). 2016. *Mental Health and Wellbeing in England: Adult Psychiatric Morbidity Survey 2014*. Leeds: NHS Digital. Retrieved 15 December 2016 from http://content.digital.nhs.uk/catalogue/PUB21748/apms-2014-full-rpt.pdf

[9]   Chip and Dan Heath. 2011. *Switch: how to change things when change is hard*. London: Random House Business Books.

[10] CALM. 2015. *42% of UK men have considered suicide*. Retrieved 28 April 2017 from http://news.thecalmzone.net/pressreleases/42-of-uk-men-have-considered-suicide-1244215

[11] Glassdoor. *About Us*. Retrieved 21 March 2017 from https://www.glassdoor.co.uk/about/index_input.htm

CHAPTER 2: YOUR EMPLOYEES

[12]   David Kravets, *Wired,* 06 March 2011 that 'U.N. report declares internet access a human right'. Retrieved 03 April 2017 from https://www.wired.com/2011/06/internet-a-human-right/

[13]   Sun Tzu. 2009. *The Art of War.* Translated by Lionel Giles (2009). Retrieved 21 March 2017 from http://classics.mit.edu/Tzu/artwar.html

[14]   Matthew D. Lieberman. 2013. *Social: Why Our Brains Are Wired to Connect,* New York: Broadway Books, Random House.

[15]   MarketInvoice. 2016. *Tips from the top: 5 lessons from Patrick Drake at HelloFresh* retrieved 21 December 2016 from https://blog.marketinvoice.com/2016/12/08/5-lessons-patrick-drake-hellofresh/

[16]   de Romrée, H., Fecheyr-Lippens, B., Bill Schaninge, B. 2016. *People analytics reveals three things HR may be getting wrong. McKinsey Quarterly.* Retrieved 21 December 2016 from http://www.mckinsey.com/business-functions/organization/our-insights/people-analytics-reveals-three-things-hr-may-be-getting-wrong

[17]   Dan Ariely. 2009. *Predictably Irrational. The Hidden Forces that Shape Our Decisions.* London: Harper Collins.

[18]   Melissa Dahl. 2016. 'How to motivate your employees: give them compliments and pizza.' *Science of Us.* Retrieved 03 April 2017 from http://nymag.com/scienceofus/2016/08/how-to-motivate-employees-give-them-compliments-and-pizza.html

[19]   Henry Stewart. 2013. *The Happy Manifesto: Make Your Organization a Great Workplace.* Great Britain: Kogan Page.

[20]   Daniel Pink. 2011. *Drive: The Surprising Truth About What Motivates Us.* New York: Canongate Books.

CHAPTER 3: YOUR CUSTOMERS

[21]   Simone Vincenzi. 2016. *Sleeping with your customers.* TEDx talk, Reading, 2016. Retrieved 11 June 2017 from https://www.youtube.com/watch?v=ay9ZBGviluA

[22]   David Taylor. 2002. *The Naked Leader: The Best Selling Guide to Unlimited Success.* London: Bantam Books.

23   Jeffrey J. Fox. 2000. *How to Become a Rainmaker*. London: Vermillion.

24   Dominic Green and Will Wei. 2013. *We Recreated The Pepsi Challenge to See What People Really Like. Business Insider.* Retrieved 21 March 2017 from http://uk.businessinsider.com/pepsi-challenge-business-insider-2013-5

25   Ted Ryan. 2011. *I'd like to buy the world a coke: the story behind the famous song*. Retrieved 21 March 2017 from http://www.coca-cola.co.uk/blog/id-like-to-buy-the-world-a-coke

26   Jonah Berger. 2014. *CONTAGIOUS. How to Build Word of Mouth in the Digital Age*. London: Simon & Schuster.

CHAPTER 4: YOUR MANAGEMENT TEAM

27   go2HR HR. 2017. *Understanding the differences: leadership vs. management*. Retrieved 21 March 2017 from https://www.go2hr.ca/articles/understanding-differences-leadership-vs-management

28   David Taylor. 2002. *The Naked Leader: The Best Selling Guide to Unlimited Success*. London: Bantam Books.

29   Sun Tzu. 2009. *The Art of War*. Translated by Lionel Giles (2009). Retrieved 21 March 2017 from http://classics.mit.edu/Tzu/artwar.html

30   Jim Collins. 2001. *Good to Great. Why Some Companies Make the Leap... and Others Don't*. London: Random House Business Books.

CHAPTER 5: YOUR POWER (THE SECRET OF HAPPINESS)

31   Mihaly Csikszentmihalyi. 2002. *Flow: The Psychology of Optimal Experience*. London: Random House.

32   Don Hellriegel and John W. Slocum. 1996. *Management. Seventh Edition*. Cincinnati: South-Western College Publishing.

33   Kraut, Pegrero, McKenna and Dunnette. 1989. 'The role of the manager: what's really important in different management jobs.' *Academy of Management Executive*. 3:286-293

34   Victor Lipman. 2013. *5 Things The Best Managers Do And Don't Do*. Retrieved 11 June 2017 from http://www.forbes.com/sites/victorlipman/2013/09/09/5-things-the-best-managers-do-and-dont-do/#1b0059ec3edd

35   Mihaly Csikszentmihalyi. 2002. *Flow: The Psychology of Optimal Experience*. London: Random House.

36   Ibid.

37   Pink, D. 2011 *Drive: The Surprising Truth About What Motivates Us*. New York: Canongate Books.

38   Ibid.

39   Ibid.

40   Jeff Haden. 2016. *8 Signs an Employee Is Exceptional (Which Never Appear on Performance Evaluations*. Retrieved 24 March 2017 from http://www.inc.com/jeff-haden/8-signs-an-employee-is-exceptional-that-never-appear-on-performance-evaluations.html

CHAPTER 6: WHO ARE YOU ANYWAY?

41   Green answering Khanh-Van Le-Bucklin (reviewer). 2000. *Why Children ask "Why"*. Retrieved 11 June 2017 from http://www.drgreene.com/qa-articles/why-children-ask-why/

42   Six Sigma Online. 2017. *Explaining The Six Sigma 5 Whys*. Six Sigma Online. Aveta Business Institute. Retrieved 11 June 2017 from http://www.sixsigmaonline.org/six-sigma-training-certification-information/explaining-the-six-sigma-5-whys/

43   iSixSigma. 2017. *Determine the Root Cause: 5 Whys*. Retrieved 11 June 2017 from https://www.isixsigma.com/tools-templates/cause-effect/determine-root-cause-5-whys/

44   TaskRabbit. 2016. Home page. Retrieved 19 December 2017 from https://www.taskrabbit.co.uk/

45   Greg McKeown. 2014. *Essentialism: The Disciplined Pursuit of Less*. Virgin Books, a division of Ebury Publishing.

46   Ibid.

CHAPTER 7: VISION AND STRATEGY

47   Chris Zook and James Allen. 2016. *The Founder's Mentality*. Harvard Business Review Press.

48   Alessio Bresciani. 2017. *51 Mission Statement Examples from The World's Best Companies*. Retrieved 02 March 2017 from http://www.alessiobresciani.com/foresight-strategy/51-mission-

49 DataScience.com. 2017. *Forrester: Companies Using Data Science Platforms Are Surpassing the Competition.* Retrieved 11 June 2017 from https://www.datascience.com/blog/forrester-research-reveals-data-science-platforms-as-competitive-differentiator

50 Jean Storlie. 2013. *Bricks, Walls, Cathedrals: A Story-bite to Lead with Vision.* Retrieved 24 March 2017 from http://www.storietelling.com/2013/08/14/bricks-walls-cathedrals-a-story-bite-to-lead-with-vision/

51 English: Oxford Living Dictionaries. 2017. Oxford University Press. Retrieved 02 March 2017 from https://en.oxforddictionaries.com/definition/strategy

52 Richard Rumelt. 2012. *Good Strategy/Bad Strategy. The Difference and Why it Matters.* London: Profile Books.

53 Max McKeown. 2012. *The Strategy Book.* Harlow: Pearson.

54 Ibid.

55 John Kotter. 2013. *When CEOs Talk Strategy, 70% Of The Company Doesn't Get It.* Retrieved 02 March 2017 from https://www.forbes.com/sites/johnkotter/2013/07/09/heres-why-ceo-strategies-fall-on-deaf-ears/#605772053663

56 James O'Gara. 2017. *Seven out of 10 Employees Don't Know Where You – Or They – Are Going.* Retrieved 02 March 2017 from https://www.itsonmessage.com/organizational-clarity-aligning-vision-strategy-story

57 Dain Dunston. 2017. *When Blockbuster Forgot What Business They Were In.* Retrieved 02 March 2017 from http://daindunston.com/when-blockbuster-forgot-what-business-they-were-in/

58 Ibid.

59 Pablo Tovar. 2016. *Leadership challenges in the V.U.C.A. world.* Retrieved 02 March 2017 from http://www.oxfordleadership.com/leadership-challenges-v-u-c-world/

60 Richard Rumelt. 2012. *Good Strategy/Bad Strategy. The Difference and Why it Matters.* London: Profile Books.

[61]   Ibid.

[62]   Ibid.

[63]   Max McKeown. 2012. *The Strategy Book*. Harlow: Pearson.

[64]   Ibid.

[65]   Omar Oakes. 2016. *One in five adults now use ad-blockers, says IAB survey*. 1 March 2016. Retrieved 14 June 2017 from http://www.campaignlive.co.uk/article/one-five-adults-use-ad-blockers-says-iab-survey/1385560

[66]   Ricardo Semler. 2004. *The Seven-Day Weekend: A Better Way to Work in the 21st Century*. London: Random House.

CHAPTER 9: GUERRILLA LEADERS

[67]   Ron Finley. 2017 Private conversation with Gina Balarin. 25 July 2017.

[68]   Ron Finley. 2013. *A guerrilla gardener in South Central LA*. Retrieved 21 December 2016 from https://www.ted.com/talks/ron_finley_a_guerilla_gardener_in_south_central_la

CHAPTER 10: FRUSTRATED STORYTELLERS

[69]   Matthew D. Lieberman. 2013. *Social: Why Our Brains Are Wired to Connect*, New York: Broadway Books, Random House.

[70]   HubSpot. *The HubSpot Culture Code*. Retrieved 20 January 2017 from http://www.slideshare.net/HubSpot/the-hubspot-culture-code-creating-a-company-we-love

[71]   Charles Duhigg. 2013. *The power of habit: Why we do what we do and how to change*. London: Random House Books.

[72]   Pablo Tovar. *Leadership challenges in the V.U.C.A world*. Retrieved 02 March 2017 from http://www.oxfordleadership.com/leadership-challenges-v-u-c-world/

[73]   Bernard Marr. 2015. *Big Data: 20 Mind-Boggling Facts Everyone Must Read*. Retrieved 18 June 2017 from http://www.forbes.com/sites/bernardmarr/2015/09/30/big-data-20-mind-boggling-facts-everyone-must-read/#5c51d8526c1d

CHAPTER 11: UNDISCOVERED IDEA-GENERATORS

[74]   Colm Gorey. 2015. *More data to be created in 2019 than in history of the internet*. Retrieved 18 June 2017 from https://www.siliconrepublic.com/comms/more-data-to-be-created-in-2019-than-history-of-the-internet

CHAPTER 12: FINDING THE HIDDEN INFLUENCERS

[75]   Gina Balarin. 2014. *Technology Marketers Meet-Up: London, June 2014*. Retrieved 18 June 2017 from https://www.brighttalk.com/webcast/43/118811

[76]   Business-comm.com. 2017. *Making Business Communication Work*. Retrieved 20 October 2017 from http://business-comm.net/newart2.html

[77]   Smriti Chand. *Communication Models: Different Communication Models as Proposed by many Management Theorists*. Retrieved 18 June 2017 from http://www.yourarticlelibrary.com/advertising/communication-models-different-communication-models-as-proposed-by-many-management-theorists/22244/

[78]   Brooke Borel. 2015. *If It Feels Like Stress Is Killing You, That's Because It Might Be*. Retrieved 20 August 2017 from http://www.popsci.com/chronic-stress-it-could-be-killing-you

CHAPTER 13: MAKING CHANGE POSSIBLE

[79]   Anon. 2017. *SWOT Analysis*. Retrieved 18 June 2017 from https://en.wikipedia.org/wiki/SWOT_analysis

[80]   Greg McKeown. 2014. *Essentialism: The Disciplined Pursuit of Less*. UK: Virgin Books, a division of Ebury Publishing.

[81]   David Taylor. 2002. *The Naked Leader: The Best Selling Guide to Unlimited Success*. London: Bantam Books.

[82]   Anon. 2016. *Supply Chain Automation, Does Change Have to be Painful?* Retrieved 18 June 2017 from https://cdn2.hubspot.net/hubfs/235257/Supply_Chain_Automation__Does_change_have_to_be_painful_final.pdf

[83]   Ibid.

84   Karl Albrecht. 2012. *The (Only) 5 Fears We All Share*. Retrieved 18 June 2017 from https://www.psychologytoday.com/blog/brainsnacks/201203/the-only-5-fears-we-all-share

85   Chip and Dan Heath. 2011. *Switch: how to change things when change is hard*. London: Random House Business Books.

CHAPTER 14: RELATIONSHIPS AND CHAMELEONS

87   Concur. *Cost-reductions due to less time spent doing expenses*. Retrieved 20 December 2017 from https://www.concur.co.uk/casestudy/pohwer

88   BlackPast.Org. *(1857) Frederick Douglass, "If There Is No Struggle, There Is No Progress"*. Retrieved 02 March 2017 from http://www.blackpast.org/1857-frederick-douglass-if-there-no-struggle-there-no-progress accessed

89   Matthew D. Lieberman. 2013. *Social: Why Our Brains Are Wired to Connect*, New York: Broadway Books, Random House.

90   Richard Templar. 2015. *The Rules of Life: A personal code for living a better, happier, more successful kind of life.* Harlow: FT Press.

CHAPTER 15: THE MARKETING STRIPTEASE

91   Dan Pink. 2014. *To Sell is Human. The surprising truth about persuading, convincing and influencing others*. London: Canongate Books.

92   Gina Balarin. 2014. *The Content Marketing Striptease*. Retrieved 23 February 2017 from http://www.cyance.com/our-blog/bid/338077/The-Content-Marketing-Striptease

93   Grace Elisabeth Cook. *9 Popular Burlesque and Cabaret Restaurants in London*. Retrieved 23 February 2017 from http://www.bookatable.co.uk/blog/burlesque-cabaret-restaurants-london

94   Krisjetz. YouTube. 2006. *1989 British Airways Commercial.* Retrieved 23 February 2017 from https://www.youtube.com/watch?v=jxs106rp5RQ

95   Kate Magee. 2015. *'You're thirsty. We've got sales targets', says Oasis in summer campaign launch.* Retrieved 23 February 2017 from

http://www.campaignlive.co.uk/article/youre-thirsty-weve-sales-targets-says-oasis-summer-campaign-launch/1353975

96   Anon. 2011. *Cravendale 'cats with thumbs' by Wieden + Kennedy.* Retrieved 18 June 2017 from http://www.campaignlive.co.uk/article/cravendale-cats-thumbs-wieden-+-kennedy/1056544

97   Gerald Chait. 2015. *'Half the money I spend on advertising is wasted; the trouble is I don't know which half.'* Retrieved 18 June 2017 from https://www.b2bmarketing.net/en-gb/resources/blog/half-money-i-spend-advertising-wasted-trouble-i-dont-know-which-half

98   Jill Rowley. *Jill (Brewbaker) Rowley. Digital Transformation | | Startup Advisor | | Affinio Board of Directors | | Speaker | | Social Selling Strategist.* Retrieved 23 February 2017 from https://www.linkedin.com/in/jillrowley/

CHAPTER 16: VOICE OF THE CUSTOMER

99   Anon. *Customer experience.* Retrieved 18 June 2017 from https://en.wikipedia.org/wiki/Customer_experience

100   Custora.com. *Retail Customer Analytics. Predictive Customer Lifetime Value Analysis.* Retrieved 18 June 2017 from https://www.custora.com/tour/feature_predictive_customer_lifetime_value_clv_retail/

101   Gina Balarin. 2015. *Why HubSpot rocks - and its customers think so too.* Retrieved 23 February 2017 from https://www.linkedin.com/pulse/why-hubspot-rocks-its-customers-think-so-too-gina-balarin

102   HubSpot.com. *HubSpot Customer Spotlight: OmPrompt.* Retrieved 23 February 2017 from https://www.hubspot.com/customers/omprompt

103   Dan Pink. 2014. *To Sell is Human. The surprising truth about persuading, convincing and influencing others.* London: Canongate Books.

104   HubSpot customer library of resources, October 2016.

105   Penquin. 2016. *Stop Fighting, Kids! The Sibling Rivalry between Sales and Marketing.* Retrieved 23 February 2017 from http://blog.penquin.co.za/blog/effective-sales-and-marketing-for-business-3-expert-perspectives

106   Gina Balarin. 2014. *Relationship counselling for sales and marketing.* Retrieved 23 February 2017 from http://www.cyance.com/our-blog/bid/347969/Relationship-counselling-for-sales-and-marketing

CHAPTER 18: PEOPLE BUY FROM PEOPLE

107   Dan Ariely. 2009. *Predictably Irrational. The Hidden Forces that Shape Our Decisions.* London: Harper Collins.

108   Malcolm Gladwell. 2006. *Blink: the power of thinking without thinking.* London: Penguin Books.

109   Gina Balarin. 2014. *B2B customer stories: How to catch that 'golden moment'.* Retrieved 18 June 2017 from https://www.b2bmarketing.net/en-gb/resources/blog/b2b-customer-stories-how-catch-golden-moment

Index

25183807R00138

Printed in Great Britain
by Amazon